# 实用大学英语(上)

主　　编：杨永华
副 主 编：钟珑菲　罗　焕　赵大艳
参编人员：陈　晶　王　娜　隆　婕　薛东梅　梁玉涓
　　　　　何楚红　韩清华　李琛莎

北京理工大学出版社
BEIJING INSTITUTE OF TECHNOLOGY PRESS

## 内容简介

《实用大学英语（上）》共8个单元。每个单元有两篇课文，分别兼顾英语的工具性和人文性。在栏目设计上，以介绍企业文化、企业产品以及业务写作等内容为主，强调以应用为目的，以"必需、够用"为编写标准。每个单元的工具性语篇都是以职场环境中的典型工作任务为主线，课文素材来源于各类英语读物，内容丰富，旨在通过各类话题的讨论和学习，帮助学生学会真实的语境交流，使他们在交流中感受真实的职业英语表达，实现思想的碰撞。

每个单元的课前讨论话题旨在方便教师在教学中引导学生从全球化的视角认识世界、了解各国不同的文化与习俗，坚定正确的人生观、价值观，以传播中华文化为己任，了解自己面对的挑战，锻炼自己的思辨能力，加强创新意识。课后的系列练习旨在加强学生对高等学校英语应用能力考试题型的熟悉。

从总体上来看，本书结构清晰、完整，难易程度安排适当，各类题型设计合理，不仅可以作为高等院校高职高专学生的英语教材，也可供各类英语爱好者学习。

**版权专有　侵权必究**

### 图书在版编目（CIP）数据

实用大学英语．上 / 杨永华主编．－－北京：北京理工大学出版社，2021.7
　　ISBN 978-7-5763-0023-9

Ⅰ．①实⋯　Ⅱ．①杨⋯　Ⅲ．①英语－高等职业教育－教材　Ⅳ．① H319.39

中国版本图书馆 CIP 数据核字（2021）第 136365 号

出版发行 / 北京理工大学出版社有限责任公司
社　　址 / 北京市海淀区中关村南大街5号
邮　　编 / 100081
电　　话 /（010）68914775（总编室）
　　　　　（010）82562903（教材售后服务热线）
　　　　　（010）68948351（其他图书服务热线）
网　　址 / http://www.bitpress.com.cn
经　　销 / 全国各地新华书店
印　　刷 / 涿州市新华印刷有限公司
开　　本 / 787毫米 × 1092毫米　1 / 16
印　　张 / 11　　　　　　　　　　　　　　　责任编辑 / 时京京
字　　数 / 297千字　　　　　　　　　　　　文案编辑 / 时京京
版　　次 / 2021年7月第1版　2021年7月第1次印刷　责任校对 / 刘亚男
定　　价 / 36.00元　　　　　　　　　　　　责任印制 / 李志强

图书出现印装质量问题，请拨打售后服务热线，本社负责调换

# 前　　言

## 一、指导思想

早在2000年10月，教育部就出台了第一部针对高职高专教育英语课程教学的指导性文件《高职高专教育英语课程教学基本要求》（以下简称《要求》），并在全国颁布实施。《要求》中明确提出了高职高专英语要"以实用为主，够用为度"的教学思想原则，其英语课程的教学目标不仅是帮助学生打好英语基础，还要为培养面向生产、建设、服务和管理第一线需要的高技能人才的目标服务。也就是强化对学生的实用英语能力训练，以培养其英语实用能力为根本，注重培养其实用英语技能，特别是培养其在未来职业中所要从事的各项业务的实用英语能力，为提高其求职竞争力和未来可持续发展打下良好基础。

《要求》提出"使学生掌握一定的英语基础知识和技能，具有一定的听、说、读、写、译的能力，从而能借助词典阅读和翻译有关英语业务资料，在涉外交际的日常活动和业务活动中进行简单的口头和书面交流，并为今后进一步提高英语交际能力打下基础"，同时，还提出对高等学校英语应用能力考试的A、B级考试［即PRACTICAL ENGLISH TEST FOR COLLEGES (LEVEL A/B)，简称PRETCO LEVEL A/B］的要求，主张加强"实用阅读"，把高等学校英语应用能力考试作为验收高职高专英语课程教学质量的标准。

《实用大学英语（上）》就是在教育部出台的《要求》指导思想下编写的。本教材以职场应用为导向，旨在培养高职高专学生职场英语应用能力，特别是基本听说能力，以帮助他们在今后的工作中能用英语有效地进行口头和书面的信息交流、增强其自主学习能力，提高综合文化素养，开阔视野，以适应职场的实际需要，同时，培养其思辨能力和创新精神。

## 二、教学对象

本套教材主要应用对象为高职高专非英语专业学生。

## 三、教材内容

全书共 8 个单元。每个单元的两篇课文分别兼顾工具性和人文性，工具性语篇都是以职场环境中的典型工作任务为主线，一般建议 4~6 个课时。每个单元里都设计有"教学目标"（Goals）、"听力练习"（Listening and Speaking）、"课前讨论"（Preview Questions）、"语法知识"（Grammar Focus）等板块。

## 四、教材特点

《实用大学英语（上）》的编写充分彰显了以下几个教学理念和特色：

### （一）培养学生的学习兴趣和国际化视野

本教材中的课文素材来源于各类英语读物，内容丰富，旨在通过各类话题的讨论和学习，帮助学生学会真实的语境交流，使他们在交流中感受真实的职业英语表达，实现思想的碰撞。Text 1 主要介绍体育运动、健康、交通等内容，Text 2 则主要以职场英语为主，分别介绍了面试、办公室事务等内容，而最后的写作训练主要是按照 B 级考试中的写作模式进行编写的，其中涵盖了通知、函电、电话、广告、海报、简历、名片等具体商务事宜。此外，课前讨论话题的设计旨在方便教师在教学中引导学生从全球化的视角认识世界，了解各国不同的文化与习俗以及自己面对的挑战，培养学生的思辨能力和创新意识。

### （二）加强实用英语学习和能力的训练

《实用大学英语（上）》强调"以教师为主导、以学生为主体"的教学理念，在每一个单元里都提出了明确的教学思路；课文内容的实用性，旨在培养学生未来的职业英语应用能力，提高学生的自学能力，尤其注重培养学生的合作能力以及信息化时代的创新能力。在栏目设计上，以介绍企业文化、企业产品以及业务写作等内容为主，强调以应用为目的，以必需、够用为度。

### （三）强化针对 A、B 级考试的全真训练

为了满足学生们检测自己英语水平和准备英语等级测试的需求，该教材在课后练习的设计上，以高等学校英语应用能力考试 A、B 级题型为主要练习题型，使学生在学习中既掌握了语言知识，又培养了学生运用英语进行有关涉外业务工作的能力，以此希望有效促进学生实际应用英语进行日常交流和涉外业务交际能力的提升，提高其在毕业生人才市场上的竞争力。

### （四）重视思政内容的课堂教学

教育部在 2020 年 6 月 1 日发布了教高〔2020〕3 号文，在《高等学校课程思政建设指导纲要》中，把课程教学中的课程思政内容提到了非常重要的位置。为了响应教育部的号召，《实用大学英语（上）》在教学目标、课文内容讨论环节设计了一些思政内容，方便教师在课堂教学中根据课文内容加入思政元素，做到英语教学中"润物细无声"的思政教学，以此在英语教学中培养学生的家国情怀，帮助学生塑造正确的世界观、人生观和价值观。思政内容紧紧围绕培养学生坚定的理想信念，"以爱党、爱国、爱社会主义、爱人民、爱集体为主线，围绕政治认同、家国情怀、文化素养、宪法法治意识、道德修养等重点优化课程思政内容供给，系统进行中国特色社会主义和中国梦教育、社会主义核心价值观教育、法治教育、劳动教育、心理健康教育、中华优秀传统文化教育"。

### （五）强化视频和网络教学平台的运用

《实用大学英语（上）》十分重视英语听说材料在教学中的运用。编者除了提供精心设计的教学课件外，还会为课程教师提供内容电子答案、音频资料和 8 套 A、B 级模拟题。

《实用大学英语（上）》主编为杨永华，副主编为钟珑菲、罗焕、赵大艳，参编人员有陈晶、王娜、隆婕、薛东梅、梁玉涓、何楚红、韩清华、李琛莎。第一至第八单元的编者为：韩清华、罗焕、何楚红、陈晶、隆婕、梁玉涓、王娜和赵大艳，模拟题第一至第八单元的编者为杨永华、薛东梅和钟珑菲。《英语 B 级考试不规则动词表》由罗焕完成，课文录音由李琛莎、陈晶完成。其中，杨永华、钟珑菲、韩清华、陈晶、薛东梅、王娜和李琛莎任职于广东科技学院，隆婕、梁玉涓任职于广州华南商贸职业学院，罗焕和赵大艳任职于广东创新科技职业学院，何楚红任职于广州南洋理工职业学院。

在本书编写过程中，编者得到了广东科技学院副校长李才教授的帮助和指导，在此表示衷心的感谢；同时，感谢广东科技学院教材科蔡文征老师在本书成书过程中所提供的帮助和指导。

由于编者水平有限，书中难免有不足之处，恳请广大读者批评指正。

《实用大学英语》编写组

# 目　录

| Unit 1 | College Life | 001 |
| Unit 2 | Sports and Health | 024 |
| Unit 3 | Job Interviews | 043 |
| Unit 4 | Office Affairs | 064 |
| Unit 5 | Internet | 083 |
| Unit 6 | Transportation | 102 |
| Unit 7 | Marketing | 120 |
| Unit 8 | Consuming Habits | 140 |
| 附录 | | 163 |

# Unit 1　College Life

**Goals**

In this unit, we will learn to:

1. talk about college life, college courses and college activities;
2. have a good command of English expressions about college life;
3. learn about an invitation letter;
4. write an invitation letter.

## Part Ⅰ　Listening and Speaking

Task 1　Look and say: Look at the following pictures and choose the right letters (A—F) to match the pictures below.

(　　)　　(　　)　　(　　)

(　　)　　(　　)　　(　　)

A. canteen	B. library	C. laboratory
D. teaching building	E. playground	F. dormitory

## Task 2 Listen and answer: You will hear two conversations. After the conversation, you will hear some questions. Choose the best answer to each question.

**Conversation 1**

1. A. schoolmates	B. teacher and student
   C. shopper and customer	D. mother and son
2. A. She has a problem in maths.
   B. She is worried about this Saturday's class.
   C. She is afraid to take part in an exam.
   D. She is worried about the speech contest.
3. A. The exam is very easy.
   B. She should be relaxed and calm and she will make it.
   C. She should play basketball to relax herself.
   D. The speech contest is not difficult.

**Conversation 2**

4. A. By travelling
   B. By doing a part-time job
   C. By studying in a training center
   D. By helping mother do housework
5. A. She has to earn money to afford her education tuition.
   B. She wants to study at home.
   C. She wants to go to visit her grandparents.
   D. She wants to learn swimming.
6. A. A swimming coach	B. A supermarket assistant
   C. A bookshop assistant	D. A salesperson

## Task 3 Listen and fill: Listen to the dialogue below twice and fill in the blanks. After listening, read the dialogue carefully and act it out with your partner.

Bill and Mike were schoolmates in a high school, and they happened to enter the same college. Bill is a sophomore and Mike is a freshman. They come across each other on campus today and now they are talking about recent college life.

Bill: Good morning, Mike, I haven't seen you for a long time. Do you enjoy your college life?

Mike: OK. But not as much as I 1 _____.

Bill: Really? Why not?

Mike: I thought that the 2 _____ would be easy and I would have lots of time to play, but actually I have much homework.

Bill: What types of homework are you having problems with?

Mike: I find my English homework very difficult.

Bill: Have you signed up for（报名参加）an English MOOC?

Mike: No, but I guess I could. Where would I find one?

Bill: You can find them on moocs.unipus.cn.

Mike: Thanks. I'll go and check that out. I wish I wouldn't get distracted by the 3 _____ games.

Bill: Oh, computer games are 4 _____. You'd better try your best to 5 _____ them.

Mike: Yes, I know, but sometimes I just find it not easy to resist（抵制）the attraction of computer games. They make me temporarily（暂时地、临时地）6 _____ especially when I feel stressed about the heavy study 7 _____ in the college.

Bill: Oh, playing computer games is not a smart way to lessen your stress. There are many 8 _____ ways to lessen your study pressures（压力）. You can join some clubs such as Photographing Club, News Report Club and Sports Club.

Mike: Cool! That sounds great! And I can also meet some new friends while taking part in the activities of the clubs. Maybe I can even make a new girlfriend. What clubs have you joined?

Bill: I joined the college Sports Club. It not only helps me build up my body but also lessens my study stress and enlarges my 9 _____ circles.

Mike: That 10 _____ fun. Are there still places open for other people to join?

Bill: Yes, they're always looking for new people to join.

Mike: Thanks. That's good to know. I'll go and sign up next week.

Bill: I'm in a hurry to the Sports Club now. Enjoy your college life. See you later.

Mike: See you later.

## Task 4  Discuss with your partner based on the mind map and make a presentation.

Is college education important? Why? How will you make the most use of college life?

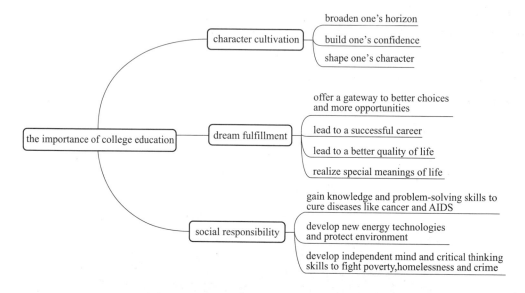

## Part II  Text 1

### Preview Questions

**Work in pairs and discuss the following questions.**

1. Do you feel anxious when you arrive at college for the first time? What problems have you met?

2. Have you ever asked for help? Whom do you turn to for help when having trouble at college?

3. What advice have you got?

### Background Information

College education is very important for a person's growth and future. The freshman year is the beginning of college life. Some students may feel like being thrown into an unfamiliar and scary situation, so they need college guidance extremely.

## How to Ease Freshman Year Worries[①]

You've made it through SAT's, applications, and FAFSA's. You are now getting ready to leave for college. While this is a very exciting time, it is also quite common for teens to feel nervous about college as they prepare to leave home for the first time. Below is a list of concerns that many teens may have and how to handle those college worries.

### Social Life

How am I going to make new friends? What if no one likes me? Who will I hang out with on the weekends?

You can be assured that all freshmen are in the same situation: they do not know anyone and also need to make new friends. Remember, this is what freshman orientation is for! Knowing this helps ease anxiety. You can research organized opportunities to kick start social interaction (such as clubs, sports, dorm activities).

What if I don't like my roommates?

For many freshmen who are nervous about college, roommates are a top concern. Many teens hope to find immediate best friend with their new roommates. This does not always happen, and that is okay! Remind yourself that your roommate does not necessarily have to be your best friend; as long as you are able to respect each other, you are on the right track. And if roommate quarrels arise, college assistants are a helpful resource.

### Studies

How am I going to get all my work done? When am I going to find the time to study?

It is important for you to be aware of the study demands and expectations at college.

---

① 本文改编自网站 Your Teen; 作者 Meredith Bonacci, PhD; 原文网址: https://yourteenmag.com/teens-college/college-life/ease-college-jitters

Chances are that it will be more challenging than your high school coursework. If you struggle with time management, let your parents or friends help you schedule in homework and study time. Have a discussion about your particular study habits and try to find the best environment on campus for your studying style.

How am I going to handle the stress? What if I get too stressed out?

Discuss with your parents or classmates what types of activities can be used to reduce stress, brainstorm the types of daily or weekly activities you can do on campus to manage stress effectively (such as yoga, running, ballgames, music). Another great way to prevent stress includes regular sleep and healthy eating habits. If there is too much stress, ask for help from psychological counseling services.

**Safety**

Will I be safe on campus?

Unfortunately, college campuses are not crime-free zones. It is important to know about safety and college security. To be careful of your surroundings and belongings, for example, it is always a good idea to use the buddy system when going out and coming home, and to lock up your valuables, even in the dormitories. Another way to stay safe is using the campus security system, for example, know where security call posts are located on campus and program the direct number in your cell phone. Make sure that parents know your class schedule, and it's always a good idea to let some classmates know where you are going and when you will return.

**New Words**（标 * 的是超纲词汇，全书同）

application/ˌæplɪˈkeɪʃn/　n. 申请，申请表；应用，运用
concern/kənˈsɜːrn/　n. 关心；担心，忧虑
handle/ˈhændl/　vt. 处理；应付
*freshman/ˈfreʃmən/　n.（大学）一年级新生
assure/əˈʃʊə(r); əˈʃɔː(r)/　vt. 确保，使确信；弄清，查明
*orientation/ˌɔːriənˈteɪʃn/　n. 方向，目标；迎新会
research/rɪˈsɜː(r)tʃ/　v. 研究；调查；探讨
opportunity/ˌɒpəˈtjuːnəti, ˌɑːpərˈtuːnəti/　n. 机会；时机
interaction/ˌɪntərˈækʃn/　n. 互动；相互影响；交互作用
resource/rɪˈsɔːrs/　n. 资源；财力；资料
*challenging/ˈtʃælɪndʒɪŋ/　adj. 挑战性的；考验能力的
*management/ˈmænɪdʒmənt/　n. 管理；管理部门
schedule/ˈskedʒuːl/　v. 安排；为……安排时间　n. 日程安排；工作计划
particular/pəˈtɪkjələ(r)/　adj. 特别的；特指的；不寻常的

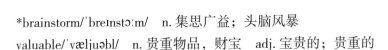

\*brainstorm/ˈbreɪnstɔːm/  n. 集思广益；头脑风暴

valuable/ˈvæljuəbl/  n. 贵重物品，财宝  adj. 宝贵的；贵重的

**Phrases and Expressions**

    hang out with   跟……一起出去玩；与……闲逛

    kick start   启动

    as long as   只要

    on the right track   在正确的道路上

    chances are that...   很有可能……

    get stressed out   压力过大；很有压力

    psychological counseling services   心理咨询服务

    crime-free zone   无罪区

    buddy-system   成对互助；结伴制

    lock up   锁上；锁起来

    security call posts   安全呼叫站

**Proper Nouns**

    SAT（Scholastic Assessment Test）学术能力评估测试

    FAFSA（The Free Application for Federal Student Aid）自愿联邦奖学金

**Notes**

    1. SAT，全称是 Scholastic Assessment Test，即学术能力评估测试，也称"美国高考"，是由美国大学理事会（College Board）主办的一项标准化的、以笔试形式进行的高中毕业生学术能力水平考试。

    2. FAFSA 是 The Free Application for Federal Student Aid（自愿联邦奖学金）的缩写，也就是我们常说的联邦学生援助，是学生申请财务帮助的一种途径。每年美国政府都会提供大量资金支付相关的教育费用，学生可以通过申请奖学金、助学金、学生贷款等形式获得相应的帮助。美国公民、国民以及拥有合法永久居留权的居民有资格申请联邦学生援助。学生需要参加 IV-eligible 项目去获得申请资格。

    3. Below is a list of concerns that many teens may have and how to handle those college worries. 这是一个倒装句，属于完全倒装。为了表达生动，有时把地点、方位副词如 up, down, out, away, below, in 等放在句首，同时把谓语动词放在主语之前（完全倒装）。若主语为人称代词，主语和谓语动词的位置不变，只将副词放在句首（不完全倒装）。如：

    Away hurried the boy. 男孩匆忙走开了。（完全倒装）

    Away he hurried. 他匆忙走开了。（不完全倒装）

    4. Chances are that it will be more challenging than your high school coursework. 这句话中的 "Chances are that..." 类似于 "It is likely that ..."，意思是"很有可能……"。

## Task 1  Answer the following questions according to the text.

1. What are the freshman's college worries?

2. What is freshman orientation for according to this text?

3. For many freshmen who are nervous about college, what are the top concern?

4. If roommate quarrels arise, who can you turn to for help?

5. What can you do to reduce stress according to the text? What other activities can you list?

## Task 2  Choose the best answer for each of the following questions or statements according to the text.

1. In the following sentence "... and to lock up your valuables, even in the dormitories", "valuables" can be replaced by _____.
    A. treasures          B. furniture
    C. importance         D. richness
2. Which of the following is not helpful in handling the stress?
    A. Regular sleep          B. Eating a lot
    C. Healthy eating habits  D. Playing ballgames
3. In order to stay safe, what should you do except _____?
    A. lock up your valuables, even in the dormitory.
    B. know where security call posts are located on campus and program the direct number in your cell phones.
    C. let some classmates know where you are going and when you will return.
    D. accept a drink from someone you don't know.
4. Which of the following sentences is true?
    A. Only few freshmen worry about making new friends on college campus.

B. You and your roommates must become best friends.

C. It's always a good idea to let your parents know your class schedule.

D. College campuses are crime-free zone.

5. What is this text mainly about?

A. Several suggestions about how to handle college worries.

B. Several suggestions about how to get along well with roommates.

C. Several suggestions about how to deal with study stress.

D. Several suggestions about how to protect yourself on campus.

## Task 3  表示具有某种职业或动作的人的名词后缀：

| 后缀 | 意义 | 举例 |
| --- | --- | --- |
| -or, -ator | 表示"……者，做……的人" | tailor, actor, author, doctor, operator, educator, professor, instructor |
| -ess | 表示"阴性人称名词" | actress, hostess, waitress |
| -ese | 表示"……国人，………地方的人" | Japanese, Cantonese, Chinese |
| -er, -eer | "从事……人，从事某种职业的人，某地区、地方的人" | banker, trainer, observer, waiter, engineer, volunteer, examiner, employer, villager, Londoner |
| -ee | 表示"动作承受者" | employee, examinee, trainee |
| -ar | 表示"……的人" | scholar, liar, beggar |
| -an, -ian, -ician | 表示"……地方的人，信仰……教的人，精通……的人，从事……职业的人" | American, Christian, historian, technician, physician, musician, electrician, magician |
| -ist, -icist | 表示"从事……研究者，信仰……主义者，……家，……者，……能手" | pianist, communist, dentist, artist, chemist, physicist, scientist |

**Fill in the blanks with the proper forms of the words given in brackets.**

1. Mary managed to find a very good driving _____ (instruct).
2. An _____ (employ) is someone who is paid to work for someone else.
3. The girl may be stupid, but she is not a _____ (lie).
4. She was studying to become a concert _____ (piano).
5. Ellen is one of our most talented young _____ (music).
6. David is a very great dramatic _____ (act).
7. She instructed the _____ (train) teacher in having classes.

8. Jack has been assigned to Italy by his _____（employ）.
9. They come from Japan. They are _____（Japan）.
10. Mike dreams to be a computer _____（operate）.

# Part Ⅲ  Grammar Focus

### 现在时态：常用的现在时态有一般现在时、现在进行时和现在完成时

**Section A  一般现在时（The Present Tense）.**

1. 一般现在时的定义及常用时间状语：在英语语法中，"时"指动作发生的时间，"态"指动作的样子和状态。一般现在时是一种英语语法形式，表示通常性、规律性、习惯性、真理性（即事实）的动作或状态。常用时间状语有 often, usually, every（day/month...）, sometimes, occasionally, from time to time, twice a week, rarely, seldom, once a month, hardly, ever, never 等。

2. 一般现在时的结构：

| 肯定式 | 疑问式 | 否定式 | 疑问否定式 | 特殊疑问句式 |
| --- | --- | --- | --- | --- |
| I work | Do I work? | I don't work | Don't I work | 特殊疑问词 when/what/how/why/where/which/who+ 一般疑问句式 |
| You work | Do you work? | You don't work | Don't you work | |
| We work | Do we work? | We don't work | Don't we work | |
| They work | Do they work? | They don't work | Don't they work | |
| He (She, It) works | Does he (she, it) work? | He (She, It) doesn't work | Doesn't he (she, it) work | |

3. 主语是第三人称单数时，动词变为相应的第三人称单数形式，变化规律如下：

| 情况 | 构成方法 | 读音 | 例词 |
| --- | --- | --- | --- |
| 一般情况 | -s | 清辅音后读 /s/ 浊辅音和元音后读 /z/ | swim-swims, help-helps, like-likes |
| 以辅音字母加 o 结尾的动词 | -es | 读 /z/ | go-goes, do-does |

续表

| 情况 | 构成方法 | 读音 | 例词 |
|---|---|---|---|
| 以 s，sh，ch，x 等结尾的动词 | -es | 读 /iz/ | watch–watches, wash–washes |
| 以辅音字母加 y 结尾的动词 | 变 y 为 i 再加 es | 读 /z/ | study–studies |
| 不规则变化 have 和 be 动词 | 变 have 为 has 变 be 为 am，is，are | | have–has, be–am, is, are |

**Task 1  Link words together into a sentence, change the form if necessary.**

Example: get up/at/six/every/Mary/morning/.

Mary gets up at six every morning.

1. always/My father/computer/plays/weekends/games/on/.

_____

2. on foot/Ken/go to school/do/not/every day/.

_____

3. do/often/Your best friend/in the playground/play/?

_____

4. don't/basketball/you/every afternoon/play/?

_____

5. move/the sun/around/the earth/.

_____

**Task 2  Take turns inquiring about activities and responding to the questions.**

Example:

A: Do you usually go to school by bus?

B: No, I don't.

A: How do you usually go to school?

B: I usually go to school on foot.

A: Why don't you go to school by bus?

B: By walking, I can exercise my body.

1. Your sister/watch TV/every day

2. Kate/buy plane tickets on the Internet/often

3. You/have breakfast at Mario's/usually
4. Your brother/travel/every year

**Section B　现在进行时（The Present Continuous Tense）.**

1. 现在进行时的定义及常用时间状语：现在进行时是英语的一种时态，表示现在进行的动作或存在的状态。现在进行时表示动作发生的时间是"现在"，动作目前的状态是"正在进行中"。现在进行时常用时间状语有 now，this week/month，right now，at the moment，these days，this term 等。

2. 现在进行时的构成：be 动词（am/is/are）+v.-ing（现在分词）

| 句式 | 现在进行时 |
| --- | --- |
| 肯定句 | 主语 +am/is/are+v.-ing 现在分词 ... |
| 否定句 | 主语 +am/is/are+not+v.-ing 现在分词 ... |
| 疑问句 | Am/Is/Are+ 主语 +v.-ing 现在分词 ...？ |
| 特殊疑问句 | 疑问代词 / 疑问副词 +am/is/are+ 主语 +v.-ing 现在分词 ...？ |

以下是动词现在分词的变化：

（1）一般在动词原形后加 ing 变成现在分词。

e.g. do–doing，sleep–sleeping，study–studying

（2）以不发音 e 结尾的动词，要去掉 e，再加 ing。

e.g. take–taking，make–making，dance–dancing

（3）以一个辅音字母结尾的重读闭音节词，要双写这个辅音字母，再加 ing。

e.g. cut–cutting，put–putting，begin–beginning

（4）以 ie 结尾的动词，把 ie 变成 y，再加 ing。

e.g. lie–lying，tie–tying，die–dying

**Task 1　Fill the blanks by using the right forms of the words in the brackets.**

1. They are _____（play）basketball now.
2. Listen，she is _____（sing）an English song.
3. We are _____（make）model planes these days.
4. It's 6:30 now. I am _____（get）up.
5. What is your brother _____（plan）to do tomorrow？

**Task 2　Make a similar dialogue like the following example.**

Example：you/do/now/read a newspaper/How often

A：What are you doing now？

B：I am reading a newspaper now.

A: How often do you read newspapers?

B: I read newspapers every morning.

1. you/do/these days/do my homework/how often
2. your father/do/now/play/who/with his friend
3. your mother/now/take a midday nap/where/in the bedroom
4. your sister/do/swim/where/in the river

**Section C  现在完成时（The Present Perfect Tense）.**

1. 现在完成时的定义及常用标志词：现在完成时是过去的动作或状态持续到现在，对现在造成影响，可能会持续发生下去。现在完成时标志词有 already, before, yet, just, recently, lately, still, never, ever, last few days, twice, up to now, so far, up to present, up till now, since+ 时间点，for+ 时间段，since+ 时间段 +ago... 等，例如：

Have they found the missing child yet?

I haven't seen much of him recently.

He has lived here since 1978.

I have been to New York three times so far.

2. 现在完成时的构成：

| 肯定句 | 否定句 | 疑问句 | 回答 |
| --- | --- | --- | --- |
| I/You have seen it. | I/You have not seen it. | Have I/you seen it? | Yes, I have.<br>No, I haven't. |
| He/She/It has seen it. | He/She/It hasn't seen it. | Has he/she/it seen it? | Yes, he/she/it has.<br>No, he/she/it hasn't. |
| We/You/They have seen it. | We/You/They have not seen it. | Have they/we/you seen it? | Yes, we/they have.<br>No, we/they haven't. |

3. 动词过去分词变化规则：

| 情况 | 构成方法 | 例词 | 读音规则 |
| --- | --- | --- | --- |
| 一般动词 | -ed | work-worked, visit-visited | 1. 动词词尾为 t, d 时，发 /id/ 音。want-wanted<br>2. 动词词尾为清辅音时，发 /t/ 音。<br>help-helped, kiss-kissed, wash-washed, watch-watched |
| 以不发音的 e 结尾的动词 | -d | live-lived, hope-hoped, move-moved, taste-tasted | |

| 情况 | 构成方法 | 例词 | 读音规则 |
|---|---|---|---|
| 以辅音字母加 y 结尾的动词 | 变 y 为 i 再加 ed | study-studied, cry-cried, carry-carried | 3. 动词词尾为 t, d 以外之浊辅音或元音时，发 /d/ 音。<br>call-called, stay-stayed, cry-cried |
| 以重读闭音节词结尾的动词，且末尾只有一个辅音字母 | 先双写该辅音字母，再加 ed | stop-stopped, ban-banned, plan-planned, drop-dropped, prefer-preferred | |

**Fill in the blanks by using the correct forms of the words in the brackets.**

1. _____ you _____ (hear) from him recently?
2. Great changes _____ (take place) since 8 years ago.
3. Peter _____ (write) six papers so far.
4. _____ they _____ (find) the missing child yet?
5. Up to the present everything _____ (be) successful.
6. Action _____ (speak) louder than words.
7. He _____ (cut) out a new letter now.
8. We _____ (learn) five hundred words up to the present.

# Part Ⅳ  Text 2

## Preview Questions

**Work in pairs and discuss the following questions.**

1. Generally speaking, how many ways are there to afford college education? How do you afford your college education tuition and college living expenses?

2. Do you feel under pressure to afford college education tuition and living expenses? If you do, how do you relieve the pressure?

## Background Information

As the government funding for education is decreasing year by year, college education tuition becomes more and more expensive. Many students have to take part-time jobs to relieve their financial burden.

## What Are Some Good College Jobs?[①]

Working while attending college is a good way to help reduce the cost of your education while gaining valuable career experience. However, not all jobs will match well with your college schedule. Seek flexible jobs that will match well with your work schedule as you progress through college.

### Tutor Fellow Students

Tutoring is a great way to help other students achieve their academic dreams while you earn some extra money. Pick a field that you feel confident in teaching, such as a foreign language or mathematics. You can use tutor networks online to advertise your services or post advertisements on bulletin boards around campus. If you're not yet ready to teach your fellow college students, consider offering your services to high school students instead.

### Babysitter

Babysitting is a good way to make money while meeting a changing schedule. If you have any neighbors or family members with young children, offer your babysitting services to them. Once you've gained some experience, you can try to use online babysitting networks to get more clients. If you babysit very young children who nap, you'll even have extra time to study for college while you're working.

### Freelance Work

Working as a freelancer gives you the opportunity to set your own hours. There are many different paths for freelance work, including writing for magazines, publishing a blog or designing websites. When you're too busy with schoolwork to meet client deadlines, you can simply stop taking new projects until you have more time.

---

① 本文改编自网站 College Choice, 08/26/2020; 作者 Staff Writers; 原文网址: https://www.collegechoice.net/college-life-3/what-are-some-good-college-jobs/

**Various Opportunities**

Keep your eyes open for one-time jobs that will give you some quick cash without a major time investment. For example, a fellow dorm resident may be willing to pay cash for people to help her move to an apartment. A local photographer may need someone to model for some pictures for an afternoon. Check online community boards and advertisements on campus for these types of opportunities.

**New Words**

*academic/ˌækəˈdemɪk/　adj. 学习的；学术的
babysit/ˈbeɪbɪsɪt/　v. 代人临时照看小孩；当临时保姆
babysitter/ˈbeɪbɪsɪtə(r)，ˈbeɪbɪsɪtər/　n. 临时保姆；代人临时照看小孩的人
*client/ˈklaɪənt/　n. 当事人；委托人；客户
*freelance/ˈfriːlæns/　adj. 特约的；自由职业的
freelancer/ˈfriːlænsə(r)/　n. 自由职业者
design/dɪˈzaɪn/　v. 设计；制图；构思；计划；筹划；制订
*deadline/ˈdedlaɪn/　n. 截止日期；最后期限
various/ˈveəriəs，ˈværiəs/　adj. 各种各样的；各种不同的
investment/ɪnˈvestmənt/　n. 投资；投资额；投资物
*resident/ˈrezɪdənt/　n. 居民；住户
photographer/fəˈtɒɡrəfə(r)，fəˈtɑːɡrəfər/　n. 摄影师；拍照者

**Notes**

1. "Working while attending college is a good way to help reduce the cost of your education while gaining valuable career experience." 本句中 v.-ing 形式的 working 是动名词做主语，while+v.-ing 形式的 attending 和 gaining 都是现在分词，表示伴随，做状语。

2. "Once you've gained some experience, you can try to use online babysitting networks to get more clients." 本句中 v.-ing 形式的 babysitting 是做定语。

## Multiple-Choice Questions

**Choose the best answer for each of the following questions or statements according to the text.**

1. According to the text, students can do the following part-time jobs except _____.
　　A. designing websites　　　　　　　B. babysitting
　　C. writing for magazines　　　　　　D. direct selling
2. Which of the sentences is not true according to the text?
　　A. Working while attending college is helpful for students to reduce the cost of education.

B. Students can only tutor high school students.

C. Students can first get some experience by babysitting the young children of neighbors or family members and then get more clients online.

D. Students can set their own hours by working as a freelancer.

3. In the sentence "If you have any neighbors or family members with young children, offer your babysitting services to them." What does "them" refer to ?

    A. Young children.

    B. Neighbors.

    C. Family members.

    D. Neighbors or family members with young children.

4. In the following sentence "You can try to use online babysitting networks to get more clients.", "clients" can be replaced by _____.

    A. purchase          B. customers          C. buy          D. babysitter

5. What is the theme of the passage?

    A. Some good college part-time jobs for students to reduce the cost of education.

    B. Tutoring fellow students.

    C. Babysitting.

    D. Freelance work.

# Part V Exercises

## Task 1 Vocabulary and Structure.

### Section A Multiple Choice.

Directions: Complete each one by deciding on the most appropriate word or words from the four choices.

1. I have an _____ to go to New York next month.

    A. challenge         B. opportunity        C. return        D. study

2. We'll go _____ the weather is good.

    A. as long as        B. as lucky as        C. as far as     D. as fast as

3. Can you show me how I can _____ the stress?

    A. define            B. handle             C. deal          D. hunt

4. The earth _____ around the sun.

    A. is moving         B. moved              C. moves         D. move

5. Mary and Kate come across each other and now they _____ about recent college life under the tree.

|   |   |   |   |
|---|---|---|---|
| A. talk | B. are talking | C. talked | D. have talked |

6. I _____ nothing from him up to now.

|   |   |   |   |
|---|---|---|---|
| A. heard | B. hear | C. am hearing | D. have heard |

7. My father _____ to the movies occasionally.

|   |   |   |   |
|---|---|---|---|
| A. goes | B. go | C. went | D. has gone |

8. We finished the task ahead of _____.

|   |   |   |   |
|---|---|---|---|
| A. manage | B. arrange | C. schedule | D. operate |

9. He has lived here _____ 1978.

|   |   |   |   |
|---|---|---|---|
| A. since | B. in | C. for | D. at |

10. I have visited the Mountain Tai five times _____.

|   |   |   |   |
|---|---|---|---|
| A. last year | B. yesterday | C. at the moment | D. so far |

**Section B　Blank Filling.**

　　**Directions：There are five incomplete statements here. You should fill in the blanks with the proper forms of the words given in the brackets.**

11. Is this man a teacher or an _____（operate）?

12. He has already _____（drop）out of college.

13. It is important for you to be aware of the study demands and _____（expect）at college.

14. My sister _____（travel）to the foreign country occasionally.

15. The parents are _____（dig）a hole on the earth to plant a tree while the children are playing.

## Task 2　Translation.

　　**Directions：This part，numbered 1 through 5，is to test your ability to translate English into Chinese. Each of the four sentences（No.1 to No.4）is followed by four choices of suggested translation marked A，B，C and D. Mark the best choice and circle the corresponding letter. Write your translation of the paragraph（No.5）in the corresponding space.**

1. You can be assured that all freshmen are in the same situation.

　　A. 你可以放心，所有大一新生都处于同样情况。

　　B. 可以肯定的是，所有大一新生都处于同样情况。

　　C. 你可以放心，所有新生情况是一样的。

　　D. 可以肯定的是，所有新生情况是一样的。

2. Many teens hope to find immediate best friends with their new roommates.

　　A. 许多青少年希望与他们的新室友成为直接的最好的朋友。

　　B. 许多青少年希望立刻与他们的新室友成为最好的朋友。

　　C. 许多青少年大学生希望立刻与他们的新室友成为最好的朋友。

D. 许多青少年大学生希望与他们的新室友成为直接的最好的朋友。

3. Keep your eyes open for one-time jobs that will give you some quick cash without a major time investment.

   A. 睁大眼睛找一份一次性的工作，这样可以让你在没有大量时间投入的情况下迅速赚到钱。

   B. 睁大眼睛找一份一次性的工作，这样可以让你在没有主要时间投入的情况下快速获得现金。

   C. 睁大眼睛找一份一次性的工作，这样可以让你在没有主要时间投入的情况下获得快的现金。

   D. 睁大眼睛找一份一次性的工作，这样可以让你在没有大量时间投入的情况下获得快的现金。

4. When you're too busy with schoolwork to meet client deadlines, you can simply stop taking new projects until you have more time.

   A. 当你因过于忙于功课而无法按时在最后期限前完成客户的交托时，你可以简单地停止新项目，直到你有更多的时间。

   B. 当你因过于忙于学业而无法在客户要求的截止日期前完成任务时，你只需停止接受新项目，直至你有更多时间。

   C. 当你忙于功课而无法按时完成客户的最后期限时，你只需停止新项目，直到你有更多的时间。

   D. 当你忙于功课而无法按时完成客户的最后期限时，你可以简单地停止新项目，直到你有更多的时间。

5. Working while attending college is a good way to help reduce the cost of your education while gaining valuable career experience. However, not all jobs will match well with your college schedule. Seek flexible jobs that will match well with work schedule as you progress through college.

_____
_____
_____
_____
_____

## Part Ⅵ Writing: Invitation Letter（邀请函/邀请信）

A. 什么是邀请函/邀请信？

邀请函/邀请信是由国家机关、社会团体、公司等单位或个人举办某些活动时，发予目标成员前来参加的邀请性质的信件。邀请函/邀请信可以是正式的，也可以是非正式的。它可以打印在纸上或通过电子邮件发送。邀请函/邀请信可用于婚礼、毕业典礼、年会、周年纪念派对和生日派对等各种活动。它还可用于邀请特邀发言人、主题发言人和研讨会主持人参加特别会议和活动。

**B. 邀请函/邀请信的内容：**

邀请函/邀请信通常包含活动的性质、内容、主办人、日期和时间、地点，发出邀请、祈求回复以及落款等。邀请函/邀请信通常在活动前几天发出，给受邀者一个回应邀请的机会。

**C. 写作范文：**

Read the letter and note the layout.

The Student Union

Qinghua University

Sept. 18, 2019

Mr. Frank Edward

Musician

Room 32, Chaoyang Road, Beijing

Dear Mr. Edward,

We are having our "Annual National Day Celebration" in the New Law Theater of Qinghua University Main Campus at 7 pm on October 1. The theme of this year's event is "Celebrating the 70th Anniversary of the Founding of China".

Would you be our guest artist？A 10-minute-to-15-minute performance will be fine.

I look forward to your favorable reply, and just as soon as I receive it, I will send you complete details. Our meeting place is New Law Theater just east of the university gate.

Yours sincerely,

David

Chairman of the Student Union

**New Words**

\*document/ˈdɒkjumənt/  n. 文件；文献；公文；证件

annual/ˈænjuəl/  adj. 每年的；年度的；一年一次的；一年的

theme/θiːm/  n. 题目，主题，主题思想

## Task 1  Multiple-Choice Questions.

**Choose the best answer for each of the following questions or statements according to the text.**

1. Which of the sentences is true？

   A. There is only formal invitation.

B. It is unnecessary to send the invitation many days in advance of the event.

C. An invitation letter can be presented to organizations or a group of people except individuals.

D. Invitation letters can be used for a variety of events such as weddings, graduation ceremonies, annual dinners, anniversary parties and birthday parties.

2. When will the event "Annual National Day Celebration" be held this year?

  A. 1th October, 2019  B. 1st October, 2019
  C. 30th September, 2019  D. September 18, 2019

3. An invitation letter usually contains the following information except＿＿＿＿.

  A. the host
  B. the date
  C. the time of the event
  D. the private time schedule of the invitee

4. In the following sentence "We are having our 'Annual National Day Celebration' in the New Law Theater of Qinghua University...", "Annual" can be replaced by ＿＿＿＿.

  A. Yearly  B. Every Year
  C. Manual  D. Anniversary

5. What is the theme of the year's event?

  A. Annual National Day Celebration
  B. Guiding and encouraging aspiring
  C. Celebrating the 70th Anniversary of the Founding of China
  D. Giving back to society

**D. 英文信函写作要点：**

（1）信头（The heading）。

信头包括发信人的地址和发信日期，写在右上角，如：

The Student Union<br>Qinghua University<br>Sept. 18th, 2019

（2）信内地址（Inside address）。

信内地址是收信人的地址，写在日期下的左上角，如：

Mr. Frank Edward

Musician

Room 32, Chaoyang Road, Beijing

（3）称呼（The salutation）。

称呼分三种情况：

A）你不知道收信人姓名：

Dear Sir,

Dear Madam,

Dear Sir/Madam,

B）你知道此人的姓氏，但他/她只和你有一般商务或学术关系：

Dear Mr.（Mrs.）Edward,

Dear Prof. Candin,

Dear Dr. Spook,

C）假如此人是你的朋友：

Dear Sue,

Dear Michael,

（4）开头语（The open sentences）。

开头语没有统一的格式，但习惯上先用客套的语句把收到对方来信的日期、主题及简单内容加以综合叙述，使对方一目了然这是答复哪一封信的。

如果是第一次通信，也可以利用开头语作必要的自我介绍，并表明目的要求。开头语一般与正文分开，自成一节，要求简单明了。

（5）正文（The body of the letter）。

正文的地位和内容与中文书信相同。在英文信函中，正文从称谓下两行起书写，行间相距一行，段落间空两行。正文以占信纸的四分之三为宜，四周留出一定空白，每行左起第一个单词要取齐，要考虑到整齐美观。

（6）结尾语（The closing sentences）。

结尾语一般用来总结文本所谈的事项，提示对收信人的要求，如"希望来信来函订货""答复询问""希望收到回信"等；另外，也附加一些略带客套的语气。正文结束后，另起一段写结尾语。

（7）结束敬语（The complimentary close）。

英文正式信函的结尾是写信人的谦称，相当于"敬上"的意思。信的敬语因人而异。

A）非常正式的公务信件：

Yours very faithfully,

Yours very sincerely,

B）正式的公务和社交书信：

Yours sincerely,

Yours truly,

Yours faithfully,

With best regards,

C）家属或亲戚的信件：

Love,

Yours affectionately,

（8）署名（The signature）

信的最后还要签名，如果信是打印的，还需要写信者亲笔落款。签名用钢笔或圆珠笔写在结尾谦称下5行的位置。

E. 实用写作：

## Task 2　Write an invitation letter according to the following information.

You are an English major in Fudan University, and you want to invite Mr. Gable, an expert on literature, to give a speech on "American literature". Write a letter of invitation on behalf of the Student Union and include the following details：

1) the purpose of the invitation；

2) the time and place of the lecture.

（相关信息：复旦大学地址是上海市杨浦区邯郸路220号，Mr. Gable 的地址是上海市徐汇区霞飞路236号。）

_____

_____

_____

_____

_____

_____

_____

_____

# Unit 2  Sports and Health

> **Goals**
> In this unit, we will learn to:
> 1. talk about sports and health;
> 2. have a good command of English expressions about sports and health;
> 3. get familiar with a notice;
> 4. write a notice about a competition.

## Part I  Listening & Speaking

**Task 1**  Look and say: Look at the following pictures and choose the right letters (A—F) to match the pictures below.

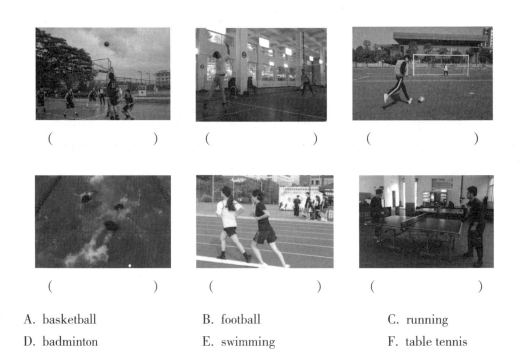

(　　　)　　(　　　)　　(　　　)

(　　　)　　(　　　)　　(　　　)

A. basketball　　　B. football　　　C. running
D. badminton　　　E. swimming　　　F. table tennis

# Unit 2　Sports and Health

**Task 2** Listen and say: You will hear two conversations. After each conversation, you will hear some questions. Choose the best answer to each question.

**Conversation 1**

1. A. Football match　　　　　　　　B. Basketball match
   C. Volleyball match　　　　　　　D. Badminton match
2. A. At 3:30 am　　　　　　　　　　B. At 3:13 am
   C. At 3:10 am　　　　　　　　　　D. At 3:30 pm
3. A. In front of Students' Dorm Building 4
   B. In front of Teachers' Dorm Building 4
   C. In front of Students' Dorm Building 5
   D. In front of Teaching Building 5

**Conversation 2**

4. A. For a month　　　　　　　　　B. For a week
   C. For a year　　　　　　　　　　D. For a term
5. A. Heath　　　　　　　　　　　　B. Study
   C. Sports　　　　　　　　　　　　D. Exercise
6. A. Play football　　　　　　　　　B. Exercise
   C. Play badminton　　　　　　　　D. Play tennis

**Task 3** Listen and act: Listen to the dialogue below twice and fill in the blanks. After listening, read the dialogue carefully and act it out with your partner.

　　　Some college students are doing sports 1 _____. They are preparing for the coming school sports meeting this week.

Lucy: Jack, will you take part in the 2 _____ of our college?

Jack: Certainly I will. I have signed up for several events, including the 200-metre race, the relay race and the high jump.

Lucy: Wow! How excellent an athlete you are!

Jack: Well, I am fond of exercise very much. I 3 _____ after school every day.

Lucy: No wonder you are 4 _____ than other students.

Jack: My roommates also like sports. We often play sports on the playground together.

Lucy: I think I should learn from you. From now on, I will do more sports. Next time you come to the playground to exercise, 5 _____ to ask me to come, too.

Jack: No problem. I am happy that I can have some influence on the people around me.

Lucy: Good luck to you in the coming sports meet.

Jack: Thanks a lot. I will try my best.

**Task 4　Discuss and role play.**

What kinds of sports do you like? Why do you like this kind of sport? When do you usually play sports? Discuss with your partner based on the mind map below and role play.

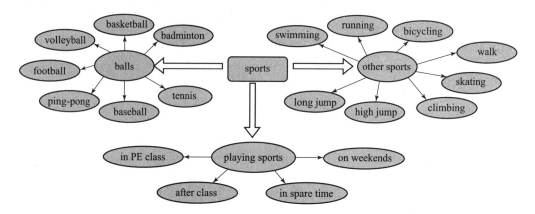

# Part Ⅱ　Text 1

## Preview Questions

**Work in pairs and discuss the following questions.**

1. Do you like playing volleyball?
2. What do you know about the Chinese women's volleyball team?
3. What can we learn from the Chinese women's volleyball team?

**Background Information**

1. Lang Ping (Dec. 10, 1960— ), head coach of the Chinese women's volleyball team, will lead this team to enter the Tokyo Olympic Games.

2. The well-known spirit of the Chinese women's volleyball team is actually a kind of never-say-die spirit, which has encouraged the team and the whole nation for many years.

## Lang Ping Biography[①]

There is little doubt that Lang Ping is one of volleyball's greats. The Tianjin-born "Iron Hammer" won two Women's World Cups, one World Championship, and an Olympic Games

---

① 本文改编自 Olympic Channel，原文网址：https://www.olympicchannel.com/en/athletes/detail/ping-lang/

gold medal as a player before becoming a widely-celebrated coach. When she led the Chinese women's team to gold at Rio 2016, she became the first person to win gold as both a player and a coach.

Lang was first selected for the Chinese national team in 1978, aged 18. Quickly becoming a mainstay of the team, the outside hitter led the Chinese team to triumph at four consecutive international championships—the 1981 and 1985 World Cups, the 1982 World Championship, and the 1984 Olympic Games. She first retired from playing in 1986, moving to the U.S. to study and coach at the University of New Mexico, but made a short return to the court a few years later during which she won World Championship silver in 1990.

Her first spell in charge as head coach of the Chinese team brought a World Cup bronze and World Championship and Olympic silver, and she was considered as a cultural icon throughout the country. Many older Chinese still associate her name with the country's booming sports in the early 1980s.

Lang took up a position with the U.S. national team in 2005 after she had been troubled over the decision for three months. Public debate was fierce in China, but Lang still accepted the job to be closer to her American-born daughter. "Now China's volleyball coaches can be 'exported' to coach in the U.S., a traditional sports power, it's an honour," she said. "There are many foreign coaches in China, so what's so odd about Chinese coaching foreign teams?"

Although she kept her Chinese citizenship, Lang was criticised in some ways when she coached the U.S. team to a win over her homeland at Beijing 2008 on the way to winning silver. But she returned to head the Chinese team in 2013, winning back those who disagreed with her decision in 2005, and success in Rio cemented her place in volleyball history.

**New Words**

  *biography/baɪˈɒɡrəfi, baɪˈɑːɡrəfi/ n. 传记；个人简介
  championship/ˈtʃæmpiənʃɪp/ n. 锦标赛；冠军称号
  medal/ˈmedl/ n. 奖牌；奖章
  *widely-celebrated/ˈwaɪdliˈselibreitid/ adj. 广受赞誉的；普遍庆祝的
  coach/kəʊtʃ/ n. 教练；长途汽车 v. 指导，作指导
  select/sɪˈlekt/ v. 选择；精选
  *mainstay/ˈmeɪnsteɪ/ n. 支柱；骨干
  *hitter/ˈhɪtə(r)/ n. 击球者；打击者
  *triumph/ˈtraɪʌmf/ n. 凯旋；胜利
  *consecutive/kənˈsekjətɪv/ adj. 连贯的；连续不断的
  retire/rɪˈtaɪə(r)/ v. 退休；离开
  court/kɔː(r)t/ n. 球场；法院；宫廷

spell /spel/ n. 一段时间 v. 拼写
*bronze /brɒnz, brɑːnz/ n. 铜
*icon /ˈaɪkɒn, ˈaɪkɑːn/ n. 偶像
associate /əˈsəʊsieɪt; əˈsəʊʃieɪt/ v. 联系；联想
boom /buːm/ n. v. 繁荣
*debate /dɪˈbeɪt/ v. n.（正式的）讨论；辩论
*fierce /fɪəs/ adj. 激烈的，猛烈的；凶猛的
export /ˈekspɔːt/ n. 出口；输出（商品）
　　　　/ɪkˈspɔːt/ v. 出口；输出
odd /ɒd, ɑːd/ adj. 奇怪的，古怪的；奇数的
*citizenship /ˈsɪtɪzənʃɪp/ n. 公民权利；公民身份
*criticise /ˈkrɪtɪsaɪz/ v. 批评
*cement /sɪˈment/ v. 巩固 n. 水泥

## Phrases and Expressions

There is little doubt that... 毫无疑问，……
outside hitter 主攻手
in charge 负责，主管
in some ways 在某些方面；在某种程度上

## Proper Nouns

Iron Hammer 铁榔头
World Cup 世界杯
World Championship 世界锦标赛
the Olympic Games 奥运会
New Mexico 新墨西哥州（美国）
Rio 里约（巴西）

## Notes

1. "There is little doubt that..." 这个句型的含义为"毫无疑问，……"。little 是一个表示否定的形容词，表示"几乎没有"，修饰名词 doubt（"怀疑、疑问"）。doubt 后面 that 所引导的是名词性从句中的同位语从句。little 也可以用 no 来代替，构成"There is no doubt that..."，同样翻译为"毫无疑问，……"。

2. Iron Hammer，即铁榔头。铁榔头是郎平的绰号。现任中国排球主教练的郎平，在 20 世纪 80 年代担任中国女子排球运动员时，一直是国家队的中流砥柱。因为她带领队友进行刻苦的训练，在球场上总是能够精准而强劲地扣杀，因此被全国人民亲切地称为铁榔头。

3. Rio 2016，指的是里约奥运会（the 2016 Rio Summer Olympic Games）。第 31 届夏

# Unit 2  Sports and Health

季奥林匹克运动会于 2016 年 8 月在巴西的里约热内卢举行。里约热内卢是第一个举行夏季奥运会的南美国家，有 207 个国家和地区的 11 544 名运动员参加了这次奥运会的比赛。

4. success in Rio，指的是中国女子排球队在郎平指导员的带领下在里约奥运会上重新登上了巅峰，获得了金牌。这也证明了"女排精神"的深入人心，又一次激励女排姑娘们去赢得成功。

## Task 1  Read the passage and judge whether the following statements are true (T) or false (F).

1. The Chinese women's volleyball team won the silver medal at the Rio Olympic Games. (  )
2. Lang Ping was the first person to win gold medals as both a volleyball player and a coach. (  )
3. She retired from playing volleyball in 1985 and moved to study and coach at the University of New Jersey. (  )
4. In 2005, the Chinese people can understand and accept the fact that Lang took up a position with the U.S. national team. (  )
5. At Beijing Olympics in 2008 the Chinese women's volleyball team won the gold medal. (  )

## Task 2  Choose the best answer for each of the following questions or statements according to the text.

1. The Rio Olympic Games was held in _____.
   A. 2008　　　　　B. 2013　　　　　C. 2016　　　　　D. 2021
2. Before becoming a head coach the U.S. national team, it took Lang Ping _____ to make a decision.
   A. three weeks　　　　　　　　　　B. three months
   C. thirteen weeks　　　　　　　　　D. thirty days
3. Lang Ping's daughter was born in _____.
   A. Beijing　　　　B. Tianjin　　　　C. America　　　　D. Rio
4. Lang took up a position with the U.S. national team in 2005 in order to _____.
   A. be closer to her daughter　　　　B. take care of her daughter
   C. earn more money　　　　　　　　D. win over the Chinese national team
5. What is this text mainly about?
   A. Lang Ping's career as a volleyball player
   B. Lang Ping's career as a volleyball coach

C. How Lang Ping works for the Chinese national team
D. The story of Lang Ping's career life

## Task 3 复合词（Compound words）：

复合词也叫合成词，是由两个或两个以上的词构成的词。构成复合词的两个词之间有时候有连字符"-"连接，有时候没有连字符。

| | 形式 | | 例词 |
| --- | --- | --- | --- |
| 复合词 | 复合名词 | n.+n. | notebook, football, classroom |
| | | v.+n. | playground, bathroom |
| | | adj.+n. | blackboard, supermarket |
| | 复合形容词 | adj.+n. | full-time, part-time |
| | | adj./n.+v.-ing | easy-going, peace-loving |
| | | adj./n.+v.-ed | kind-hearted, man-made |
| | 复合副词 | | outdoors, anywhere, downtown |
| | 复合代词 | | someone, nobody, anything |
| | 复合动词 | | underline, overcome |

According to the word formation above, please match the words in Column A with the words in Column B to form compound words.

| Column A | Column B |
| --- | --- |
| 1. no | A. ship |
| 2. text | B. consuming |
| 3. widely | C. self |
| 4. citizen | D. side |
| 5. how | E. built |
| 6. time | F. thing |
| 7. in | G. ground |
| 8. her | H. ever |
| 9. back | I. celebrated |
| 10. newly | J. book |

# Part Ⅲ　Grammar Focus

## 过去时态（The Past Tense）

过去时态包括一般过去时、过去进行时和过去完成时。

**Section A　一般过去时（the Simple Past Tense）.**

1. 一般过去时的定义：一般过去时表示过去发生的动作或存在的状态，常与表示过去的时间状语连用，如 yesterday（昨天），the day before yesterday（前天），last week（上个星期），last year（去年），two days ago（两天前），just now（刚才），once upon a time（从前），in 2008（在 2008 年）……

2. 一般过去时的构成：使用动词过去式。be 动词表示状态，过去式是 was（单数）和 were（复数）。行为动词表示动作，过去式的规则变化加后缀 ed 构成。

以下是动词过去式的规则变化：

（1）一般在动词原形后加 ed 变成过去式。

e.g. look–looked, work–worked, call–called

（2）以不发音 e 结尾的动词，直接加 d 变成过去式。

e.g. hope–hoped, believe–believed, improve–improved

（3）以辅音字母加 y 结尾的动词，把 y 改成 i，再加 –ed。

e.g. study–studied, reply–replied, copy–copied

（4）以一个辅音字母结尾的重读闭音节词，要双写这个辅音字母，再加 ed。

e.g. stop–stopped, plan–planned, copy–copied

注意：要了解不规则动词的过去式，请看附录中的《英语 B 级考试不规则动词表》。

The little boy <u>stopped</u> crying and went to sleep.（动作）
　　　　　　规则动词的过去式

Once upon a time there <u>was</u> a beautiful princess.（状态）
　　　　　　不规则动词的过去式

Lang Ping <u>won</u> World Championship silver in 1990.（动作）
　　　　　　不规则动词的过去式

**Section B　过去进行时（the Past Continuous Tense）.**

1. 过去进行时的定义：过去进行时表示过去某一时刻或者某一阶段正在发生的动作，常与 then（那时），at that time（那时，在那个时候），all day（整天），the whole morning（整个早上），at nine last night（昨晚九点），last weekend（上个周末）等时间状语连用。when+ 一般过去时的时间状语从句表示当……的时候……

2. 过去进行时的构成：be 动词（was/were）+v.–ing（现在分词）。was 用于单数，were 用于复数。关于动词原形怎么变成现在分词，可以参考 Unit 1 的语法内容。

They were discussing the problem in the meeting room then.（过去某一时刻）

I was practising playing badminton these days.（过去某一阶段）

### Section C  过去完成时（the Past Perfect Tense）.

1. 过去完成时的定义：过去完成时可以表示在过去某一时间之前已经完成的动作或状态，也可以表示从过去某一时间开始一直持续到过去另一时间的动作或状态。常用的时间状语有：long before（很久以前），by that time（到那时为止），by the end of last month（到上个月底为止）。when+ 一般过去时的时间状语从句表示当……的时候……

2. 过去完成时的构成：had+v.-ed（过去分词）。规则动词的过去分词的变化同过去式。

注意：要了解不规则动词的过去分词，请看附录中的《英语 B 级考试不规则动词表》。

The train had left when I got to the railway station.

Lang Ping took up a position with the U.S. national team in 2005 after she had been troubled over the decision for three months.

She had lived in Dongguan City for eight years before she became a professor.

### Task 1  Find out and underline the tenses in the following sentences and tell which past tenses they belong to.

1. We had much in common and gradually became close friends.
2. By the end of last term, I had taken twelve courses.
3. He borrowed some books from the library last week.
4. The college student was doing a part-time job for a restaurant the whole summer vacation.
5. It was too cold in the winter of 1999.
6. The hard-working girl had studied at the university for a year and a half when I met her for the first time.
7. They were preparing for the important examination at that time.
8. When I arrived home, my mother had made a wonderful cake for me.

### Task 2  Choose the correct answer.

1. We _____ a wonderful romance film together last weekend.
   A. see          B. saw          C. have seen          D. had seen
2. We _____ a wonderful action movie together this time last weekend.
   A. were seeing  B. saw          C. have seen          D. had seen
3. We _____ the science fiction movie three times because it is really wonderful.
   A. see          B. saw          C. have seen          D. had seen
4. When he reached the cinema, we _____ the wonderful cartoon film.
   A. see          B. saw          C. have seen          D. had seen
5. The old man _____ his coat and went out to have a walk.

A. put    B. putted    C. has put    D. had put

6. The little girl _____ the zither （古筝） for three years before she became a junior high school student.

   A. studied
   B. has studied
   C. had studied
   D. was studying

7. The little girl _____ the zither when we came into the room.

   A. studied
   B. has studied
   C. had studied
   D. was studying

8. The environment in this area _____ seriously six years ago.

   A. polluted
   B. was polluted
   C. were polluted
   D. had been polluted

## Task 3  Make the words together into a sentence and pay attention to the past tenses.

1. having a party/they/her/by/last night/birthday/celebrated/.

_____

2. all day/papers/roommates/were writing/my/the/.

_____

3. by/the papers/all night/were being written/roommates/my/.

_____

4. the task/by/yesterday morning/nine o'clock/she/had finished/.

_____

# Part Ⅳ  Text 2

## Preview Questions

**Work in pairs and discuss the following questions.**

1. Do you like swimming? Why?
2. Do you think swimming is good for people? What are the benefits of swimming?

**Background Information**

Swimming is a kind of important sport, which is very popular with people. We can swim outdoors or indoors as long as there are rivers, lakes and swimming pools, etc. Actually, swimming does good to our health, so we should learn to swim.

# The Benefits of Swimming: the Reasons Why You Should Learn to Swim[①]

Swimming is a fun and great way to stay fit and active with much lower impact on your joints than other aerobic sports.

Regular swimming can offer anyone, particularly elderly people, a wide range of health benefits. The following are the benefits of swimming.

**Full body exercise**

Swimming uses all the body's muscles so whether you swim for fun or fitness, you will get full body exercise. Swimming is also really helpful as a way to stretch out your whole body as you keep reaching further out with your strokes.

**Maintain a healthy weight**

Swimming is one of the best ways to keep your weight under control. An average swim can burn over 200 calories in just 30 minutes. As a general rule, for every 10 minutes of swimming: the breast stroke will burn 60 calories; the backstroke torches 80; the freestyle lights up 100; and the butterfly stroke incinerates 150 calories.

**Reduce heart disease risk**

Swimming aids the heart in pumping more efficiently thus ensuring a better blood flow throughout your body.

An analysis by *The Annals of Internal Medicine* showed that regular aerobic exercise such as swimming could reduce blood pressure and improve heart health.

Additionally, the American Heart Association reports that just 30 minutes of exercise per day, such as swimming, can reduce coronary heart disease in women by 30~40 percent.

**Reduce stress**

Swimming is also a best exercise for relieving stress. The contact with the water is very beneficial in helping to loosen up the body and mind. The regular rhythm of the stroke, the immersion in the water and the concentration on the technique quickly feel like a relaxing meditation in the water. Research also shows that swimming can reverse damage to the brain from stress.

---

① 本文改编自 eHealthzine, 作者: Hezy Evans, 原文网址: https://www.ehealthzine.com

## Live longer

A new study suggests that swimming may offer life-extending benefits. For the study, researchers at the University of South Carolina followed 40,547 men, aged 20 to 90, for 32 years.

The data showed that those who swam had a 50 percent lower death rate than runners, walkers or men who got no exercise. The study authors concluded that the same benefits would be received by women as well as men.

## New Words

joint/dʒɔɪnt/　n. 关节；结合处
*aerobic/eəˈrəʊbɪk/　adj. 有氧的；需氧的
muscle/ˈmʌsl/　n. 肌肉
fitness/ˈfɪtnəs/　n. 健康；合适
maintain/meɪnˈteɪn/　v. 维持；维修
control/kənˈtrəʊl/　n.v. 控制，支配；管理
*calory, calorie/ˈkælərɪ/　n. 卡路里（热量单位）
*backstroke/ˈbækstrəʊk/　n. 仰泳
*freestyle/ˈfriːstaɪl/　n. 自由泳；自由式
*incinerate/ɪnˈsɪnəreɪt/　v. 烧成灰；焚化
aid/eɪd/　v. n. 帮助；援助
*pump/pʌmp/　v. 抽吸；打气
ensure/ɪnˈʃʊə(r)/　v. 保证；确保；担保
additionally/əˈdɪʃənəli/　adv. 此外；加之
*coronary/ˈkɒrənri/　n. 冠的；冠状的
stress/stres/　n. 压力；紧张
*beneficial/ˌbenɪˈfɪʃl/　adj. 有益的；有利的
*loosen/ˈluːsn/　v. 放松；松开
*rhythm/ˈrɪðəm/　n. 节奏；韵律
*immersion/ɪˈmɜːʃn/　n. 沉浸；陷入；专心
concentration/ˌkɒnsnˈtreɪʃn, ˌkɑːnsnˈtreɪʃn/　n. 集中；专心
*meditation/ˌmedɪˈteɪʃn/　n. 冥想；沉思
*reverse/rɪˈvɜː(r)s/　v. 颠倒；撤销；反转
*life-extending　adj. 生命延续的，延长寿命的
data/ˈdeɪtə; ˈdɑːtə/　n. 数据（datum 的复数）；资料

## Phrases and Expressions

stay fit　保持健康
impact on　对……的影响；对……的作用

elderly people  老年人；老人家
a wide range of  大范围的；多种多样的
stretch out  伸直；伸出四肢
breast stroke  蛙泳
butterfly stroke  蝶泳
blood flow  血流；血流量

**Proper Nouns**

the Annals of Internal Medicine  内科医学年鉴，内科学年鉴
the American Heart Association  美国心脏协会，美国心脏学会
the University of South Carolina  南卡罗来纳大学

**Notes**

游泳最常见的方式有四种：自由泳（freestyle）、蛙泳（breast stroke）、蝶泳（butterfly stroke）、仰泳（backstroke）。除此之外，还有狗刨、潜泳、蹼泳，等等。

## Multiple-Choice Questions

**Choose the best answer for each of the following questions or statements according to the text.**

1. Swimming can make you keep fit because of the reasons except that _____.
   A. it can exercise your full body
   B. it can reduce your stress
   C. it can reduce all your diseases
   D. it can make you live longer

2. Regular swimming can do good to the health of _____.
   A. the young people
   B. the old people
   C. the sick people
   D. all the people above

3. An average swim can burn over _____ calories in half an hour.
   A. 200            B. 60            C. 80            D. 100

4. Swimming, can reduce _____ in women by 30–40 percent.
   A. coronary lung disease                B. coronary heart disease
   C. COVID-19                             D. COVID-20

5. Which of the following is NOT a type of swimming?
   A. breast stroke                        B. stroke
   C. freestyle                            D. backstroke

## Part V  Exercises

### Task 1  Vocabulary and Structure.

**Section A  Multiple Choice.**

Directions: Complete each one by deciding on the most appropriate word or words from the four choices.

1. There is no doubt _____ the opportunity of working in this corporation is attractive.
    A. how  B. when  C. that  D. what
2. The Beijing Olympic Games _____ in 2008.
    A. held
    B. were held
    C. was held
    D. are held
3. She doesn't like to associate _____ this sort of people.
    A. with  B. to  C. in  D. at
4. Those _____ suffer from COVID-19 are not taken good care of in that county.
    A. that  B. what  C. which  D. who
5. When I arrived at the airport, the plane _____ .
    A. took off
    B. taken off
    C. had taken off
    D. was taking off
6. Playing sports regularly _____ good _____ our health.
    A. is...to
    B. is...for
    C. are...to
    D. was...for
7. The customer as well as his friends _____ the considerate service of the company.
    A. benefit
    B. benefit from
    C. benefits
    D. benefits from
8. Your preparation has an important impact _____ how you will perform in an interview.
    A. in  B. on  C. of  D. at
9. Swimming is one of the best _____ to keep your weight under control.
    A. way  B. a way  C. ways  D. waies
10. We suggest that you _____ the sales manager to complain about the product.
    A. contact
    B. would contact
    C. contacting
    D. to contact

**Section B  Blank Filling.**

Directions: There are five incomplete statements here. You should fill in the blanks with the proper forms of the words given in the brackets.

1. _____ (additional), swimming can reduce heart disease risk.
2. As a general rule, for every 10 minutes of swimming the breast stroke will burn 60 _____ (calory).
3. Most of the students _____ (concentration) on the English teacher's lecture at that time.
4. The girl is crazy about _____ (fit), but her family can't understand her.
5. The people who sleep early at night can live much _____ (long) than those who stay up too late.

## Task 2  Translation.

Directions: This part, numbered 1 through 5, is to test your ability to translate English into Chinese. Each of the four sentences (No.1 to No.4) is followed by four choices of suggested translation marked A, B, C and D. Mark the best choice and circle the corresponding letter. Write your translation of the paragraph (No.5) in the corresponding space on the Sheet.

1. Swimming is a fun and great way to stay fit and active with much lower impact on your joints than other aerobic sports.
    A. 游泳是保持身体健康有活力的一种有趣的好方法,对关节的影响比其他有氧运动要小得多。
    B. 游泳可以保持身体健康有活力,可以成为一种有趣的好方法,对关节的影响比其他有氧运动要小得多。
    C. 因为对关节的影响比其他有氧运动要小得多,所以游泳是保持身体健康有活力的一种有趣的好方法。
    D. 虽然对关节的影响比其他有氧运动要小得多,但是游泳是保持身体健康有活力的一种有趣的好方法。

2. Additionally, the American Heart Association reports that just 30 minutes of exercise per day, such as swimming, can reduce coronary heart disease in women by 30–40 percent.
    A. 美国心脏协会附加报道说,每天运动30分钟(比如游泳)能够让妇女患冠心病的概率降低30%~40%。
    B. 此外,美国心脏协会报道说,每天运动30分钟(比如游泳)能够让妇女患冠心病的概率降低到30%~40%。
    C. 另外,美国心脏协会报道说,每天运动30分钟(比如游泳)能够让妇女患冠心病的概率降低30%~40%。
    D. 美国心脏协会报道说,每天附加运动30分钟(比如游泳)能够让妇女患冠心病的概率降低到30%~40%。

3. Although she kept her Chinese citizenship, Lang was criticised in some ways when she coached the U.S. team to a win over her homeland at Beijing 2008 on the way to winning silver.
   A. 虽然郎平保留了她的中国国籍，但当她教导美国队在北京 2008 年奥运会被她的祖国打败，获得银牌时，她在某些方面受到了批评。
   B. 虽然郎平取消了她的中国国籍，但当她教导美国队在北京 2008 年奥运会打输了，获得银牌，而她的祖国获得金牌时，她在各方面受到了批评。
   C. 虽然郎平取消了她的中国国籍，但当她指导美国队在北京 2008 年奥运会打赢了，而她的祖国却仅获得银牌时，她在某些方面受到了批评。
   D. 虽然郎平保留了她的中国国籍，但当她指导美国队在北京 2008 年奥运会获得了金牌，而她的祖国却仅获得银牌时，她在某些方面受到了批评。

4. Many older Chinese still associate Lang Ping's name with China's booming sports in the early 1980s.
   A. 许多中国老人一说起郎平的名字，就想起 20 世纪 80 年代早期中国体育运动的繁荣。
   B. 许多年老的中国人还是把郎平的名字和 20 世纪 80 年代早期中国体育运动的繁荣联系起来。
   C. 许多年纪大一些的中国人仍然把郎平的名字和 20 世纪 80 年代早期中国体育运动的繁荣联系起来。
   D. 许多年纪大一些的中国人仍然喜欢提起郎平的名字和 20 世纪 80 年代早期中国体育运动的繁荣。

5. A new study suggests that swimming may offer life-extending benefits. For the study, researchers followed 40,547 men, aged 20 to 90, for 32 years. The data showed that those who swam had a 50 percent lower death rate than runners, walkers or men who got no exercise. The study authors concluded that the same benefits would be received by women as well as men.

# Part Ⅵ　Writing: Notice（书面通知）

### A. 什么是书面通知？

A notice is a sort of practical writing with written or printed information, which is frequently put in a public place. It is used to inform people of something that is going to happen or something that has happened. The factors of a notice include the main activity, the time, the place and the background information, etc. The notice can be made good use of on campus to declare the change of a schedule, to have or cancel a class or a meeting, to carry out or put off an activity, etc.

Sample writing:

December 16th, 2020

### B. Sample writing:

## NOTICE

In order to inspire more college students to play more sports and keep healthy, we are going to hold the ninth sports meeting of our college from this Thursday to this Friday. All athletes of different departments should be well organized and prepared to participate in the events of the meeting. The opening ceremony of this meeting will be held on the great playground at 7:00 a.m. on Thursday, December 19th, 2020. The president, the deans, the leaders, the celebrities and the faculty will be present at the sports meet. Moreover, there is going to be various wonderful performances at the opening ceremony. Welcome to join us!

the Students' Union

### New Words

*inspire/ɪnˈspaɪər/　v. 鼓励；激发
athlete/ˈæθliːt/　n. 运动员；选手
department/dɪˈpɑːtmənt/　n. 部门；系
*dean/diːn/　n. 院长；系主任
*celebrity/səˈlebrəti/　n. 名人；名流
*faculty/ˈfæklti/　n. 全体教员
*moreover/mɔː(r)ˈəʊvə(r)/　adv. 而且；此外

### Phrases and Expressions

participate in　参加
opening ceremony　开幕式
be present at　出席

the Students' Union 学生会（=the Student Union）

**Answer the following questions:**

1. What's the purpose of having the school sports meeting?
2. How long will the school sports meeting?
3. When will the opening ceremony of the school sports meet take place?
4. Where is the opening ceremony be held?
5. Who will be present at the opening ceremony?

**C. 书面通知写作要点：**

书面通知通常包括标题、中文、时间、落款几个部分。

（1）标题（The title）。

在第一行正中间写上"NOTICE"。为了醒目，每一个字母都要大写。

e.g.                           **NOTICE**

也可以在第一行的右边写上日期，把"NOTICE"放在第二行。

e.g.                                              Feb. 22nd, 2021

**NOTICE**

（2）正文（The body）。

正文包括具体的人物（who）、事件（what）、时间（when）、地点（where）也就是"四 W"。在正文中还可以指出相关活动的具体内容和注意事项。

（3）落款（The close）。

落款通常是发通知的单位，通常写在正文的右下方。

e.g.                                              the Student Union

注意：书面通知的语言必须简明扼要，易于理解。因为书面通知是通知大家关于将来的事情，所以通常使用一般将来时。书面通知的注意事项常常会对被通知者提出一些要求，所以习惯使用祈使句。

**D. Practical Writing.**

Task 1  假如你们学校准备举行一场篮球比赛，比赛双方是外语系和财经系的球员。比赛将于六月十日（星期四）下午三点至四点在学校的体育馆举行。请代表外语系写一份书面通知（notice），欢迎师生们来参观比赛。

Task 2  假如你们学校准备举行一场篮球比赛，比赛双方是外语系和财经系的球员。由于有些设施出现故障，你们本来计划于六月十日下午三点在学校的体育馆举行的篮球比赛需要推迟到六月十五日下午四点举行。请代表外语系写一份书面通知（notice），及时告知师生们比赛日程的改变。

# Unit 3　Job Interviews

**Goals**

In this unit, we will learn to:
1. talk about jobs and interviews;
2. have a good command of English expressions on job interviews;
3. get familiar with a recruitment ad and a resume;
4. write a resume.

## Part Ⅰ　Listening and Speaking

**Task 1**　Look and say: Look at the following pictures and choose the right letters (A—F) to match the pictures below.

(　　　)　　(　　　)　　(　　　)

(　　　)　　(　　　)　　(　　　)

A. chef   B. lawyer   C. reporter
D. dancer   E. security guard   F. doctor

## Task 2  Listen and say: You will hear two conversations. After each conversation, you will hear some questions. Choose the best answer to each question.

**Conversation 1**

1. A. The interviewee   B. The interviewer
   C. The manager   D. The boss
2. A. The company is in decline.   B. The company is small.
   C. The company sells electronic products.   D. The company sells daily goods.
3. A. He will recommend Mary for the job.
   B. He will introduce the job to Mary.
   C. He is going to spend the time in doing the research.
   D. He is not going to hire Mary.

**Conversation 2**

4. A. He will have a job interview.
   B. He will be confident.
   C. He is going to spend the time in doing the research.
   D. He will behave well.
5. A. He is worried about his appearance.
   B. He is worried about making the interviewer angry.
   C. He is worried about his ability.
   D. He is worried that he will fail the interview.
6. A. To wear nice clothes   B. Take it easy and be himself
   C. Take the interview seriously   D. Pretend to be experienced

## Task 3  Listen and fill: Read the dialogue below carefully and discuss with your partner about job interview.

Mark: First of all, please tell me about your 1 _____ _____.

Lily: OK. I graduate from Hainan Vocational College. 2 _____ _____ is computer application.

Mark: OK. What kind of personality do you think you have?

Lily: Well, I am fond of learning new things. And I'm a 3 _____ _____ _____ person.

Mark: What do you think are your advantages and disadvantages?

Lily: I'm a little careless. But I 4 _____ _____ _____ this problem, so I'm trying to be more careful in my work. I think my advantages are that I am 5 _____ and good at learning.

Mark: Why do you choose our company?

Lily: First, my major meets the requirements of your position. Second, I think your company can provide me with 6 _____ for growth. At the same time, I can 7 _____ _____ to your company.

Mark: Are there any questions you'd like to ask?

Lily: Do you provide 8 _____ _____ to employees?

Mark: Yeah. We select excellent employees to 9 _____ _____ training programs in Germany every year. Do you have any interest in this?

Lily: Sure. If I can work in this company, I will 10 _____ _____ _____.

## Task 4  Discuss and debate.

How do you answer interview questions in a proper way and impress the interviewer? Discuss with your partner according to the mind map below.

```
I graduate from...
My major is...  →  ①Education                    ④Why do you choose our company?  →  First, my major...
                                                                                      Second, I think your company...
I am a/an+adj.+person
I am(adj.)...   →  ②Personalities  →  Interview  →  ⑤Your questions about the job  →  Salary
                                      Questions                                        Training Programs
                                                                                       Opportunities
I am...
My advantages/disadvantages are  →  ③Advantages and disadvantages                   ⑥Other questions  →  What do you think of...
                                                                                                          Why should we hire you?
```

# Part Ⅱ  Text 1

## Preview Questions

**Work in pairs and discuss the following questions.**

1. How many kinds of jobs do you know? Please list them down.
2. What do you want to do in the future?
3. How would you prepare for an interview for the job you dream to do?

## Background Information

The interview is the most important stage in your whole job search process. The success or failure of an interview depends on your performance in just a few minutes. Everyone is able to learn how to perform in an interview perfectly. And most mistakes can be predicted and avoided. The following are the tips to bring you a chance to succeed.

# Things that Ruin Your Perfect Interview[①]

No matter how perfect your resume is, if you mess up a job interview you won't get that position. In today's tough economy you need every possible edge. Here are things to do that will dramatically increase your chances.

### Don't be a "smiley face."

Excessive smiling in a job interview is seen for what it is—nervousness and a lack of confidence. A smiley-face person exudes phoniness, which will quickly be picked up by the interviewer. Instead be thoughtful and pleasant. Smile when there's something to smile about. Do a practice run in front of a mirror or friend.

### Don't be a small-talker

Your job is to be knowledgeable about the company for which you're interviewing. Random facts about last night's episode of "Dancing with the Stars" or your favorite blog will not get you the job. Never feel you have to fill an interview with small talk. Find ways to talk about serious subjects related to the industry or company. Pockets of silence are better than padding an interview with random babble.

### Don't sweat

You can lose a job by wearing an undershirt or simply a little too much clothing. Sweaty palms or beads on your forehead will not impress. You are not applying to be a personal trainer. Sweat will be seen as a sign of weakness and nervousness. Do a practice run with your job interview outfit in front of friends. The job interview is one place you definitely don't want to be hot.

### Don't be a road block

Interviewers are seeking candidates eager to take on challenging projects and jobs. Hesitance and a nay-saying mentality will be as visible as a red tie and seen as a negative. Practice saying "yes" to questions about your interest in tasks and work that might normally give you pause.

---

① 本文改编自可可英语网站；原文网址：http://www.kekenet.com/read/201003/99286.shtml

**Don't be petty**

Asking the location of the lunchroom or meeting room will clue the interviewer into your lack of preparation and initiative. Prepare. Don't ask questions about routine elements or functions of a company: where stuff is, the size of your cube, and company policy on coffee breaks.

**Don't be a liar**

Studies show that employees lie frequently in the workplace. Lying won't get you a job. In a job interview even a slight exaggeration is lying. Never stretch your resume or embellish accomplishments. There's a difference between speaking with a measured confidence and engaging in BS. One lie can ruin your entire interview, and the skilled interviewer will spot the lie and show you the door.

**New Words**

  resume/ˈrezjumeɪ, rɪˈzjuːm, rɪˈzuːm/ n. 个人简历；履历
  interview/ˈɪntəvjuː/ n. 采访；面试
  increase/ɪnˈkriːs/ v. 增加；增大；提高
  confidence/ˈkɒnfɪdəns, ˈkɑːnfɪdəns/ n. 信心；信任
  practice/ˈpræktɪs/ n. 实践；练习
  relate/rɪˈleɪt/ v. 涉及；与……有某种联系
  impress/ɪmˈpres/ v. 给予某人深刻印象
  apply/əˈplaɪ/ v. 申请
  *weakness/ˈwiːknəs/ n. 弱点；软弱
  *definitely/ˈdefɪnətli/ adv. 清楚地；明确地
  challenge/ˈtʃælɪndʒ/ v. 挑战；考验
  *visible/ˈvɪzəbl/ adj. 明显的；看得见的
  negative/ˈneɡətɪv/ adj. 消极的；否定的
  preparation/ˌprepəˈreɪʃn/ n. 预备；准备
  initiative/ɪˈnɪʃətɪv/ n. 主动权；首创精神
  measure/ˈmeʒə(r)/ v. 测量；估量
  engage/ɪnˈɡeɪdʒ/ v. 从事；参与
  ruin/ˈruːɪn/ v. 破坏；糟蹋

**Phrases and Expressions**

  no matter 不管；不论
  mess up 陷入困境；搞糟
  a lack of 缺乏；缺少
  pick up 捡起；获得

fill...with...　用……填满……
related to　涉及；有关
apply to do　申请做
see...as...　把……看作……；视……为……

**Notes**

1. No matter your resume and talents, if you mess up a job interview you won't get that position. 不管你有什么样的简历和才华，如果在面试上砸了，你就无法得到那个职位。"no matter"意为"不论、不管"，引导让步状语从句。

2. Random facts about last night's episode of "Dancing With the Stars" or your favorite blog will not get you the job. 昨晚电视节目《星随舞动》的内容或你最喜爱的博客等话题都不会让你得到这份工作。《星随舞动》（Dancing With the Stars）是美国ABC电视台于2005年夏天推出历时八周的舞蹈比赛类真人秀节目，是美国收视第二高的真人秀节目，受大众喜爱。本句借此生动幽默地表明面试时不要讲与工作无关的闲话。

3. Pockets of silence are better than padding an interview with random babble. 片刻间歇的沉默比用胡言乱语填充面试要更好。pockets of 表示"一些，零星"。random babble 表示"胡言乱语"。"are better than"是比较级，意为"比……更好，胜过"，表示前者胜过后者。本句采用比较级表明沉默比胡言乱语要好。

4. Hesitance and a nay-saying mentality will be as visible as a red tie and seen as a negative. 犹豫和拒绝的心态将会是赫然醒目，并被视为消极的信号。"as...as"意为"和……一样"，是同级比较，表示两个事物的性质或程度相当。本句用同级比较，表示"hesitance and a nay-saying mentality"（犹豫和拒绝的心态）和"red tie"（红领带）一样明显，赫然醒目。

5. One lie can ruin your entire interview, and the skilled interviewer will spot the lie and show you the door. 一个谎言会破坏全部面试，有经验的面试者一定会发现那个谎言，让你离开。"spot"作动词有"认出、发现"的意思，"spot the lie"即"识别谎言"。本句中"show you the door"并不是字面含义的"向你展示门"，而是表示"让你离开"。这也不难理解，其实在中国文化里请人离开时，也会用"门在那边"来表达。

## Task 1　Answer the following questions according to the text.

1. What will happen if you mess up the job interview?

2. Why shouldn't you be a "smiley face" in the job interview?

3. What could sweat be seen as?

4. What kind of candidates are interviewers seeking?

5. What would the skilled interviewer do if you tell a lie?

## Task 2  Choose the best answer for each of the following questions or statements according to the text.

1. When shall you smile in an interview?
   A. When there's something to smile about
   B. When others smile
   C. When you think you shall smile
   D. When the interviewer is smiling

2. Which of the following is true?
   A. You can know little about the company you're interviewing.
   B. Talking about "Dancing with Stars" will get you the job.
   C. Find ways to talk about the company.
   D. Silence is worse than random babble.

3. Which best explains the meaning of the underlined phrase "road block"?
   A. Saying "yes" to tasks and work
   B. To take on challenging projects and jobs
   C. Hesitance and a nay-saying mentality
   D. To wear a red tie

4. Which of the following is the question about the routine elements or the functions of a company?
   A. The size of the cube
   B. Where stuff is
   C. Company policy on coffee break
   D. All above

5. What is this passage mainly about?
   A. How to please the interviewer.
   B. Tips on how to behave in a job interview.
   C. How to be polite in a job interview.
   D. Do not lie in a job interview.

## Task 3  名词后缀：

| 后缀 | 意义 | 举例 |
| --- | --- | --- |
| -age | 多加在动词、形容词后表示"……的动作或结果" | shortage |

续表

| 后缀 | 意义 | 举例 |
|---|---|---|
| -ure | 表示"动作（过程）；状态" | closure, explosure |
| -al | 表示"……的动作" | arrival |
| -dom | 在表示"……的状况"时，构成不可数名词 | freedom |
| -ance, -ence | 表示"……的动作（过程、状况等）" | appearance, existence |
| -ism | 指"……主义；学说；……行为；（动作）过程" | criticism |
| -ion, -(a)tion | 多与动词结合构成名词，表示"行为（动作或其过程的）结果" | election, completion |
| -ness | 多与形容词结合，构成名词，表示"……（的）状态、性质、程度" | kindness |
| -hood | 表示"……状态；……时期" | manhood |
| -ship | 表示"身份、地位、资格；（……期间的）状况" | membership |
| -ty, -ity | 表示"特性、状态" | regularity |

According to the word formation above, please match the suffixes in column A with the words in column B.

| Column A | Column B | Column A | Column B |
|---|---|---|---|
| 1. -age | A. equality | 8. -ion | H. failure |
| 2. -ure | B. foundation | 9. -(a)tion | I. childhood |
| 3. -al | C. criminal | 10. -ness | J. coldness |
| 4. -dom | D. competence | 11. -hood | K. expansion |
| 5. -ance | E. idealism | 12. -ship | L. reliance |
| 6. -ence | F. wisdom | 13. -ty | M. friendship |
| 7. -ism | G. marriage | 14. -ity | N. beauty |

## Part Ⅲ  Grammar Focus

### 将来时态（The Future Tense）[①]

将来时态包括一般将来时、过去将来时和将来完成时。

**Section A  一般将来时（The Simple Future Tense）.**

1. 一般将来时的定义：表示将来某时的动作或状态，或将来某段时间内经常发生或出现的动作或状态，常与表将来的时间状语连用，如：tomorrow（明天），the day after tomorrow（后天），next time（下一次），next week（下周），soon（不久，很快），in the future（将来，在未来），in+ 一段时间等。

2. 一般将来时的构成：主要有四种常见的结构。

（1）will/shall+ 动词原形，表示将来某时将要发生的动作或存在的状态。需注意 will 可用于各种人称，shall 只用于第一人称。否定则在 will/shall 后加 not。

e.g. Grandma will give me a birthday present next month.

奶奶下个月会送生日礼物给我。

We shall complete this project next week.

我们将在下周完成本项目。

（2）be going to+ 动词原形，表示计划、安排和打算要做的事。"be going to" 相当于一个助动词，与动词原形一起构成谓语。需注意 "be" 有人称和数的变化。

e.g. He is going to buy flowers this afternoon.

他打算今天下午去买花。

（3）现在进行时表将来。表位置移动的动词，如 go, come, start, move, leave, arrive 等，可用现在进行时表示即将发生的动作。

e.g. We are arriving in Guangzhou.

我们即将抵达广州。

（4）在 when（当……的时候），as soon as（一……就……）引导的时间状语从句和 if（如果），unless（如果不、除非）引导的条件状语从句中，要用一般现在时表示

---

[①] 将来时态源于百度百科；

一般将来时原文网址：https://baike.baidu.com/item/%E4%B8%80%E8%88%AC%E5%B0%86%E6%9D%A5%E6%97%B6

过去将来时原文网址：https://baike.baidu.com/item/%E4%B8%80%E8%88%AC%E8%BF%87%E5%8E%BB%E5%B0%86%E6%9D%A5%E6%97%B6?fromtitle=%E8%BF%87%E5%8E%BB%E5%B0%86%E6%9D%A5%E6%97%B6&fromid=3452695

将来完成时原文网址：https://baike.baidu.com/item/%E5%B0%86%E6%9D%A5%E5%AE%8C%E6%88%90%E6%97%B6

将来。

  e.g. When he grows up, he will become a scientist.

  等他长大，他要当一名科学家。

### Section B　过去将来时（The Past Future Tense）.

  1. 过去将来时的定义：过去将来时表示从过去的某一时刻来看将要发生的动作或呈现的状态。

  2. 过去将来时的构成：主要有四种常见的结构。

  （1）"would/should+ 动词原形"构成过去将来时，常表示将要发生的事。需注意 would 可用于各种人称，而 should 只用于第一人称。

  e.g. He said he would support me.

  他说他会支持我。

  My grandpa said we should overcome the difficulties.

  我爷爷说我们会渡过难关。

  （2）"was/were +going to + 动词原形"表示过去根据计划或安排即将发生的事。

  e.g. Mr. Smith said he was going to visit Tom this evening.

  史密斯先生说他今晚要去看汤姆。

  （3）表示位置移动的动词，如 go, come, start, move, leave, arrive 等，可用过去进行时表示过去即将发生的动作。

  e.g. Lily told me that she was leaving for Shenzhen.

  莉莉告诉我她要去深圳。

  （4）在 when（当……的时候），as soon as（一……就……）引导的时间状语从句和 if（如果），unless（如果不、除非）引导的条件状语从句中，要用一般过去时表示过去将来。

  e.g. I didn't know when John would call, but when he called I would inform you.

  我不知道约翰什么时候会来电话，但他来电话时我会通知你。

### Section C　将来完成时（The Future Perfect Tense）.

  1. 将来完成时的定义：将来完成时是用在表示在将来某时以前已完成或一直持续的动作。

  2. 将来完成时的构成：将来完成时的结构为 shall（第一人称）或 will（各种人称）+ have+ 过去分词（done）。主要有三种用法。

  （1）表示在将来某时之前已完成的动作，并往往对将来某一时间产生影响。

  e.g. Let's meet at eight tomorrow evening. I will have finished the work by then.

  我们明天晚上八点见面，到时我已经完成工作了。

  （2）表示猜测，相当于"must have done"结构。

  e.g. I'm certain that the train will have arrived in Tianjin tomorrow evening.

  我肯定火车明天晚上就到天津了。

（3）表示某种状态一直持续到说话人所提及的时间。

e.g. Mr. Smith will have worked here for ten years by next year.

到明年，史密斯先生在这里工作就满十年了。

## Task 1　Put the right forms in the brackets.

1. Call me tomorrow. I _____（be）at home then.
2. Dad asked me if I _____（come）home.
3. By the end of this week, we _____（finish）this task.
4. He _____（buy）some flowers this afternoon.
5. By the end of this winter, Lily _____（save）5,000 yuan.
6. Did you know whether Mike _____（come）to the party?
7. Jack _____（work）here for 6 years by next month.
8. I _____（go）to college in the future.
9. It _____（snow）soon.
10. A new university _____（build）here next year.

## Task 2　Choose the correct answer.

1. I wish you _____ the task before I come back tomorrow.
   A. will finish              B. finishes
   C. will have finished       D. has finished
2. Alice said that she _____ me next week.
   A. visit                    B. would visit
   C. will visit               D. is visiting
3. I didn't know whether Lily _____ tomorrow morning.
   A. would come     B. comes     C. come     D. came
4. —Would you like to join our team?
   —Yeah. _____ .
   A. I'll be glad             B. I'll like
   C. I'd love                 D. I'd love to
5. There _____ a lecture this afternoon.
   A. will be going to         B. will going to be
   C. is going to be           D. will go to be
6. Tom _____ here next year.
   A. is working               B. isn't working
   C. has worked               D. will work
7. Grandpa _____ me a present next month.

A. will give  B. will gives  C. gives  D. give

8. By the end of this summer, John _____ here for two years.

   A. will live  B. lives

   C. live  D. will have lived

9. By the end of this year, I _____ two books.

   A. will read  B. will have read

   C. reads  D. am reading

10. All the programs _____ by the end of this month.

    A. will complete  B. will have been completed

    C. will have completed  D. is going to complete

## Task 3  Link words together into a sentence.

1. week/free/next/will/be/he/.

_____

2. it/going/rain/is/soon/to/.

_____

3. he/promised/would/that/he/me/support/.

_____

4. next week/have/finished/will/he/by/the task/, /.

_____

# Part Ⅳ  Text 2

## Preview Questions

**Work in pairs and discuss the following questions.**

  1. Where can you see recruitment ads（招聘广告）?

  2. What kind of recruitment ads have you seen?

  3. What are the requirements of the position in these recruitment ads?

**Background Information**

We are one of the world's largest, non-athletic shoe brands. We have one hundred and eighty years of shoe-making history and are constantly adopting new innovative ways of manufacturing and selling shoes. Now we are recruiting a Project Management Assistant. The requirements for this position are as follows:

## Wanted[①]

Position:

Project Management Assistant

Responsibility:

——Provide service for the project in Chongqing.

——Provide assistance to the project manager for everyday work.

Requirements:

——College degree and above.

——Good English and computer skills.

——Related working experience in the international organization.

Contact information:

——Tel: 9707-6565123

——E-mail: Mark Zhang@163.com

**New Words**

  position/pəˈzɪʃn/   n. 位置；职位

  management/ˈmænɪdʒmənt/   n. 管理；经营

  responsibility/rɪˌspɒnsəˈbɪləti, rɪˌspɑːnsəˈbɪləti/   n. 责任；职责

  provide/prəˈvaɪd/   vt. 提供；准备

  assistance/əˈsɪstəns/   n. 援助；帮助

  requirement/rɪˈkwaɪəmənt/   n. 要求；需求

  degree/dɪˈɡriː/   n. 程度；等级

  international/ˌɪntəˈnæʃnəl/   adj. 国际的；世界的

  contact/ˈkɒntækt, ˈkɑːntækt/   n. 接触；联系

**Phrases and Expressions**

  (be) responsible for   对……负责

  provide...for/to...   把……提供给……

**Multiple-Choice Questions**

**Choose the best answer for each of the following questions or statements according to the text.**

1. What position is being recruited?

  A. Project Management Assistant    B. Manager

  C. Salesman    D. Lawyer

---

[①] 本文改编自宜昌韦博英语；原文网址：https://www.qinxue365.com/yyxx/597915.html

2. Which of the following is the responsibility of this position?
   A. Provide goods for the project
   B. Provide service to manager
   C. Provide service to the project in Chongqing
   D. Responsible for selling goods
3. Which of the following is NOT the requirement of this position?
   A. College degree and above
   B. Good English and computer skills
   C. Related working experience
   D. Working independently
4. How to contact them if you are interested in this position?
   A. Send an E-mail to Mark Zhang@qq.com
   B. Call the number 9707-6565123
   C. Be one of their customers
   D. Get a college degree

# Part V   Exercises

## Task 1   Vocabulary and Structure.

**Section A   Multiple Choice.**

   **Directions: Complete each one by deciding on the most appropriate word or words from the four choices.**

1. A good plan can lead you through every _____ of your life.
   A. stage          B. round          C. start          D. memory
2. Jack is responsible _____ fixing computer problems.
   A. in             B. for            C. at             D. on
3. She seems to _____ by the birthday present.
   A. surprise                         B. surprises
   C. surprised                        D. be surprised
4. It is _____ a charming car that we are all attracted by it.
   A. so             B. such           C. too            D. also
5. Mom promised to give me a present. She failed _____.
   A. either         B. but            C. too            D. though
6. Rose is a nice girl and she never____ requests of others.
   A. turns off                        B. turns down

C. turns up   D. turns in

7. _____ I say, he won't listen to me.

   A. wherever   B. however   C. whatever   D. whenever

8. The clothes _____ her 100 yuan.

   A. cost   B. spent   C. taken   D. paid

9. _____ got up earlier, they wouldn't miss the bus.

   A. Had they   B. Would they   C. They had   D. They would

10. Tom had an _____; he fell down the stairs yesterday.

    A. issue   B. business   C. accident   D. event

**Section B   Blank Filling.**

**Directions**: There are five incomplete statements here. You should fill in the blank with the proper forms of the words given in the brackets.

11. I think this clock needs to _____(repair).

12. It is high time they _____(take) some actions.

13. I forget _____(bring) the umbrella this morning.

14. He _____(spend) a lot of time on study, so that he got good grades.

15. This rule is _____(particular) important to us.

## Task 2   Translation.

**Directions**: This part, numbered 1 through 5, is to test your ability to translate English into Chinese. Each of the four sentences (No. 1 to No. 4) is followed by four choices of suggested translation marked A, B, C and D. Mark the best choice and circle the corresponding letter. Write your translation of the paragraph (No. 5) in the corresponding space.

1. When they realize that you are a stranger, they will help you with enthusiasm and care.

   A. 当他们知道到你是一个陌生人时，他们就会热情地对你。

   B. 当他们意识到你是一个陌生人时，他们就会热情和关心地帮助你。

   C. 当他们意识到你是一个人时，他们就会冷淡地对你。

   D. 当他们意识到你是一个陌生人时，他们就会热心地对你。

2. Students at Peking University will offer calligraphy classes for children.

   A. 四川大学的学生将为儿童提供舞蹈课。

   B. 北京大学的学生将为儿童提供书法课。

   C. 儿童上了北京大学的学生提供的书法课。

   D. 儿童将上四川大学的学生提供的舞蹈课。

3. If we want to keep our health and strong body, eating habits play an important role in our life.

   A. 如果想锻炼我们身体，饮食习惯在我们的生活中起着很重要的作用。

   B. 如果想保持我们的健康，饮食习惯在我们的生活中不太重要。

C. 如果想保持我们的健康和强壮的身体，饮食习惯在我们的生活中起着很重要的作用。

D. 如果想拥有健康，作息习惯在我们的生活中起着很重要的作用。

4. According to the terms of this contract, if you are not satisfied with anything, you have the right to amend it.

A. 根据本合同条款规定，如果你有什么不满意的地方，你有权力提出修改。

B. 如果你有什么满意的地方，你无权提出修改。

C. 如果你有什么不满意的地方，你可以提出修改。

D. 根据本合同条款规定，如果你有什么不满意的，你无权力提出修改。

5. With the process of economic globalization, business communication between people becomes more frequent. Business English has turned into the working language globally, and has attracted people's great attention.

_____
_____
_____
_____
_____
_____

# Part Ⅵ  Writing: Resume（简历）

**A. 什么是简历？**

简历是对个人学历、经历、特长、爱好及其他有关情况所作的简明扼要的书面介绍。简历是有针对性的自我介绍的一种规范化、逻辑化的书面表达。对应聘者来说，简历是求职的"敲门砖"。

**B. 简历的基本内容**

简历主要由四个基本内容组成：

1. 基本情况：姓名、性别、出生日期、婚姻状况和联系方式等。

2. 教育背景：按时间顺序列出学历、所就读学校、专业和主要课程。所参加的各种专业知识和技能培训。

3. 工作经历：按时间顺序列出参加工作至今所有的就业记录，包括公司/单位名称、职务、就任及离任时间，应该突出所任每个职位的职责、工作性质等，此为求职简历的精髓部分。

4. 其他：个人特长及爱好、其他技能、专业团体、著述和证明人等。

下面是一个简历的样本。

## C. Sample:

| | Resume | | | |
|---|---|---|---|---|
| Name | Mark Smith | Date of Birth | 1996.05 | |
| Gender | Male | Marital status | single | |
| E-mail | Mark Smith@163.com | Tel | 123456 | Photo |
| Address | Beijing Road, Guangzhou City, Guangdong Province, China | | | |
| Objective | Manager Assistant | | | |

❖ Educational Background

2005.07—2009.06    TJ Vocational College

Majoring in product operation

Main courses taken in:

Management, Microeconomics, Management Information System, Statistics, Accounting, Financial Management, Economic Law, International Marketing

❖ Work Experience

- 2009—2010 Guangzhou Huaxu LTD. Manager Assistant

Reception of clients, arranging the meeting

- 2008—2009 volunteer in the Beijing Olympic Games

Receive foreign guests

❖ Skills

Mandarin grade A; Cet-4/CET-6 (good listening, speaking, reading and writing skills);
National Computer Rank Examination Level 2; proficient in Microsoft Word, Excel and Power point.

❖ Personalities

Outgoing, positive, creative and hardworking

❖ Hobbies

Going hiking, reading, table tennis

## Task 1  Discuss the following questions with your classmates.

1. Do you think it is important to write a good resume when looking for a job?
2. What shall we do to make a resume more attractive?
3. What information should a resume include?

## Task 2  Answer the following questions about the sample above.

1. What is the educational background of Mark Smith?
2. Where has Mark Smith worked and what are his duties?
3. What skills does Mark have?

**D. Useful patterns.**

1. Education.

2005—2009  ×××college   majoring in  ×××

Main courses：…

2. Work experience.

Start with the most recent employment：

- 2009—2010  Guangzhou Huaxu LTD．Manager Assistant

Reception of clients，arranging the meeting

- 2008—2009 volunteer in the Beijing Olympic Games

Receive foreign guests

3. Skills.

- Computer abilities：

Familiar with/Proficient in Microsoft Office    熟悉/精通软件办公

- Language skills：

Fluent in…/A good command of…    ……流利/精通……

Passed CET-4/CET-6 通过大学英语四级/六级考试

- Abilities related to your major

Skilled in…  擅长……

With a certificate in…  有……证书

Accounting Professional  会计专业人士

4. Hobbies.

oil painting，table tennis，Chinese chess，boxing，go hiking，etc.

油画、乒乓球、象棋、拳击、远足等。

5. Personalities.

honest，independent，outgoing，active，energetic，open-minded，etc.

诚实、独立、外向、积极、精力充沛、思想开放等。

## Task 3  Fill in the blanks of the resume with the words below.

| CET-6 | Main courses | Address |
| Resume | Work Experience | Chinese chess |

| | | 1_____ | |
|---|---|---|---|
| Photo | Name: Lily Taylor<br>2_____ : Guangzhou, Guangdong<br>Date of Birth: 1995.1.1 | | Objective: Media PR<br>Telephone: 12345678910<br>E-mail: 123456789@qq.com |
| | | Educational Background | |
| 2014—2016 | South China University of Technology, majoring in Human Resource Management | | |
| 3_____ : Management, Microeconomics, Macroeconomics, Management information System, Statistics Accounting, Financial Management, Marketing, Western economics, Human resources management. | | | |
| | | 4_____ | |
| 2015—2016 | Dongguan Huayang Network Technology LTD. HR administrative intern<br>Main duties: conducting initial interviews with candidates; Write the candidate report; assisting the superior to check and manage the fixed assets of the office and the mobile assets; Responsible for the supervision and implementation of the rules and regulations | | |
| | | Skills | |
| 5_____ , Accounting Professional Qualification Certificate | | | |
| | | Personalities | |
| frank, independent and outgoing | | | |
| | | Hobbies | |
| table tennis, 6_____ | | | |

## Task 4  Try to write a resume according to the following information.

John Smith is going to graduate from Guangzhou University. He plans to find a job so he needs to write a resume now. Please write a resume of John based on the following information.

姓名：约翰史密斯

地址：广东广州

出生日期：1995年1月1日

求职意向：市场销售员

联系电话：12345678910

电子邮箱：123456789@qq.com

教育背景：

2010—2014　广州大学　市场营销　本科学历

工作经历：

2014年6—9月　广州电器有限公司　市场销售员

主要职责：销售公司电器产品

技能特长：

CET-6、会计从业资格证书

性格：

乐观开朗、善于学习、乐于助人

兴趣爱好：

喜欢羽毛球、篮球、音乐、看书

# Unit 4    Office Affairs

**Goals**

In this unit, we will learn to:

1. talk about working from home, office supplies and office affairs;
2. have a good command of English expressions on office affairs;
3. get familiar with a memo;
4. write a memo.

## Part I    Listening & Speaking

**Task 1    Look and say: Look at the following pictures and choose the right letters (A—F) to match the pictures below.**

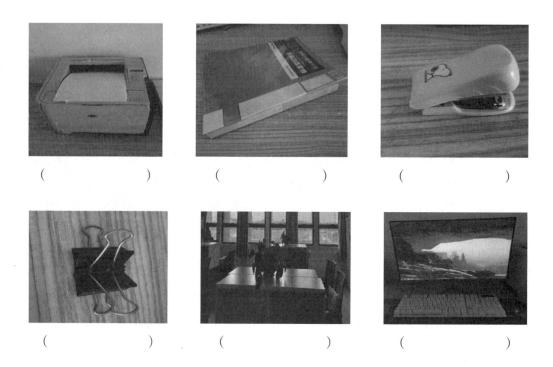

(            )        (            )        (            )

(            )        (            )        (            )

A. computer  B. stapler  C. folder
D. printer  E. cubicles  F. clip

## Task 2  Listen and say: You will hear two conversations. After each conversation, you will hear some questions. Choose the best answer to the questions.

**Conversation 1**

1. A. She feels cold.  B. She caught a cold.
   C. She likes cold weather.  D. She caught a fever.
2. A. Because she needs the man's help.
   B. Because she is very glad.
   C. Because she wants to hear his voice.
   D. Because she wants to take the day off.
3. A. Teacher and student  B. Father and daughter
   C. Employer and employee  D. Classmates

**Conversation 2**

4. A. Because she has worked overtime for three weeks.
   B. Because she has finished her report.
   C. Because she can't get extra money.
   D. Because she doesn't like her job.
5. A. Because he likes to work overtime.
   B. Because he needs to get the money.
   C. Because he has a report to finish.
   D. Because his boss asked him to work overtime.
6. A. Extra money  B. Experience
   C. Praise  D. Joy

## Task 3  Listen and fill: Read the dialogue below carefully and discuss with your partner: Is it a good idea for employees to speak up their ideas to their boss directly? ①

Lucy: Jason, do you have a 1 _____? I'd like to ask you about something.
Jason: Sure. What is it?
Lucy: I think you can give me some 2 _____. You have worked here longer, and I just want to know what you think.

---

① 本文改编自网站学习啦；时间 2020.4.28,；原网址：https://www.xuexila.com/english/xiaqingjing/c396083.html

Jason: I'm glad to help you. But what is it you want to ask about?

Lucy: I am worried about the meeting this morning.

Jason: Why? I think the meeting went well.

Lucy: Really?

Jason: Yes. But what are you worried about?

Lucy: I'm afraid I was too 3 _____.

Jason: Why would you think like that?

Lucy: Well, maybe I talked to Mr. Henry too 4 _____. I thought maybe I said too much. I don't want him to be angry.

Jason: I understand. But you said what you thought. I think he 5 _____ that.

Lucy: Really?

Jason: Yes.

Lucy: But I am new here and he is the 6 _____ of the company. I'm not sure he is 7 _____ that.

Jason: Listen, Lucy. You shouldn't worry about Mr. Henry. He is a very good man to work for. He appreciates people for their ideas.

Lucy: I am very happy to hear that, Jason. It's good to know I'm working in such a company.

Jason: I 8 _____ with you on that, Lucy. I've worked for Mr. Henry for nine years up to now. I feel he appreciates his 9 _____ for their work. I would never change jobs.

Lucy: Good. Thank you for telling me this.

Jason: Any time. If you have a good idea, don't be afraid to speak up. This is a company that appreciates 10 _____.

## Task 4  Discuss and debate.

People have different ideas towards working from home. Do you think it's a good choice or bad choice for employees to work from home?

Less Communication with Co-workers
No Separation between Work and Life
Work doesn't End with Too Much Temptation
Difficulty in Getting Promoted

Working from Home

No Commuting
Flexible Working Time
Less Distractions
More Contact with Family Members

# Part Ⅱ　Text 1

## Preview Questions

**Work in pairs and discuss the following questions.**

1. Do you prefer working at the office or working from home?
2. What kind of office would you like to work in?

**Background Information**

After the outbreak of COVID-19, more and more companies ask their employees to work from home, which makes people wonder whether it's still necessary to go back to their offices. Will companies give up their offices? The following text will give you some hints.

## The Office of the Future[①]

Over the last couple of months, the world has taken a course on "working from home" (WFH). While not without its challenges, one thing has proven itself to be true. We can do it. Many companies who traditionally occupy offices within the city's downtown center have their employees working in bedrooms and kitchens, and in some cases resulting in a better productivity.

So, why have offices at all? Why not take those costs and put them into more robust digital work systems? Give everyone a killer home-tech setup, a comfy chair and away you go.

But working from home isn't for everyone. It's true that digital workspaces give us flexibility, however, this new set-up lacks the magic of in-person collaboration. The office of the future must focus on balancing the digital world and the real world.

The office of the future must give people a compelling reason to visit it. It must offer all the things that home offices do not. Connection and collaboration. Amenities and entertainment. We need spaces and activities that bring people together, invigorate corporate culture, and provide health or cultural benefits.

Now more than ever, we need dynamic spaces for us to work. Yes, we all need meeting rooms where we can bounce ideas off each other and feel inspired by each other's creative energy. But we also want gyms, theaters, libraries, stages, gardens—spaces that make our work lives and personal lives feel symbiotic.

---

① 本文改编自网站 Riza；时间 2020.5.30；原网址：https://rize.ca/think/the-office-of-the-future/

We are all undergoing a reevaluation. Some of us have fallen in love with working from homes, having the flexibility of time and cutting down on daily commutes. While others are yearning to be back into offices where they can create a separation between their home life and work life. One thing is certain, the demand for more thoughtful and dynamic office spaces will change the culture of work.

**New Words**

  *occupy/ˈɒkjupaɪ, ˈɑːkjupaɪ/ vt. 占据，占领；使忙碌；居住
  *productivity/ˌprɒdʌkˈtɪvəti/ n. 生产率；生产力
  *robust/rəʊˈbʌst/ adj. 强健的；健康的；粗野的；粗鲁的
  digital/ˈdɪdʒɪtl/ adj. 数字的；手指的 n. 数字；键
  *comfy/ˈkʌmfi/ adj. 舒服的；轻松的
  *flexibility/ˌflɛksəˈbɪləti/ n. 柔韧性；机动性，灵活性
  *collaboration/kəˌlæbəˈreʃən/ n. 合作；协作
  *compelling/kəmˈpɛlɪŋ/ adj. 引人入胜的；非常强烈的；令人信服的
  *amenity/əˈmɛnəti/ n. 舒适；礼仪；愉快；便利设施
  entertainment/ˌentəˈteɪnmənt/ n. 款待；娱乐
  *invigorate/ɪnˈvɪɡəret/ vt. 使生气勃勃
  dynamic/daɪˈnæmɪk/ adj. 动态的；有活力的 n. 动态；动力
  inspire/ɪnˈspaɪə/ vt. 鼓舞；激发；启示；产生；使产生灵感
  *symbiotic/ˌsɪmbaɪˈɒtɪk, ˌsɪmbaɪˈɑːtɪk/ adj. 共生的
  *commute/kəˈmjʊt/ vi. 通勤
  *yearn/jɜː(r)n/ vi. 渴望

**Phrases and Expressions**

  in some cases  在某些情况下；有时候
  result in  导致
  focus on  关注
  corporate culture  企业文化
  cut down  削减

**Notes**

  1. Over the last couple of months, the world has taken a course on "working from home". course 意为"进程、航向"，本句意为过去数月以来，世界踏上了"在家工作"这一进程。这指的是在全球新冠肺炎疫情爆发的背景下，世界各国的民众纷纷开始采取"在家工作"的工作模式。

  2. not without its challenges，其中 not without 为双重否定，意为肯定，表示前文提

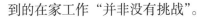

到的在家工作"并非没有挑战"。

3. Give everyone a killer home-tech setup, a comfy chair and away you go. 本句当中的 killer 本意为"杀手",在这里用来修饰 setup,指的是"杀手级别"或"精英级别"的设备;comfy chair 即"舒适的椅子",在这里代指舒适的工作环境。"away you go"为倒装用法,原本顺序为"you go away"。在英语当中,方位介词或副词提前,后面的句子要完全倒装。例如"Here comes the bus."。本句意为只要公司为员工提供在家办公所需的良好设备和舒适的椅子(代指工作环境),你(指公司)就可以万事大吉了。

4. while others are yearning to be back into offices 中 while 除了表示"当……时候",相当于 when,还表示"然而",多用于前后两者进行对比。

## Task 1  Answer the following questions according to the text.

1. Is it good for companies to ask their employees to work from home?

2. Can every company choose WFH?

3. What are the disadvantages of WFH?

4. What will future offices be like if they want employees to visit them?

5. What are people's attitudes toward working from home?

## Task 2  Choose the best answer for each of the following questions or statements according to the text.

1. According to the author, what's the result of companies choosing WFH?
   A. All of them will have a better productivity.
   B. Most of them will have a better productivity.
   C. Some of them will have a better productivity.
   D. Only a few of them will have a better productivity.

2. What should future office focus on?
   A. Digital world

B. Reality life

C. Balance of digital world and real world

D. Feeling of employees

3. Which is NOT right about the office of the future compared with WFH?

   A. It can bring people together.

   B. It can invigorate company culture.

   C. It can provide health benefits.

   D. It can create better productivity.

4. What is for sure about the future office?

   A. Employees will fall in love with it.

   B. Employees will cut down their daily commutes.

   C. It can create separation between home life and office life.

   D. The demand for office space will change the culture of work.

5. What is this text mainly about?

   A. An introduction of WFH

   B. An introduction of the future office

   C. The advantages of WFH

   D. The advantages of the future office

## Task 3　名词的复数形式（Plural Forms of Nouns）：

| 一、以 f 和 fe 结尾的单词　规则：变 f 或 fe 为 "ves" | | | | | |
|---|---|---|---|---|---|
| 单数 | 复数 | 词义 | 单数 | 复数 | 词义 |
| wolf | wolves | 狼 | wife | wives | 妻子，太太 |
| half | halves | 半个 | knife | knives | 小刀，刀子 |
| calf | calves | 小牛 | life | lives | （个人的）性命 |
| sheaf | sheaves | 捆，束，扎 | thief | thieves | 贼 |
| leaf | leaves | 叶子 | | | |

| 二、结尾是 o 的单数词，一部分只加 s 就成复数词 | | | | | |
|---|---|---|---|---|---|
| 单数 | 复数 | 词义 | 单数 | 复数 | 词义 |
| piano | pianos | 钢琴 | photo | photos | 照片，相片 |
| radio | radios | 收音机 | bamboo | bamboos | 竹子 |
| zoo | zoos | 动物园 | kangaroo | kangaroos | 袋鼠 |

# Unit 4　Office Affairs

续表

### 三、结尾是 o 的有生命力的词，一般加 "es" 口诀：黑人英雄吃西红柿马铃薯

| 单数 | 复数 | 词义 | 单数 | 复数 | 词义 |
| --- | --- | --- | --- | --- | --- |
| negro | negroes | 黑人 | hero | heroes | 英雄 |
| tomato | tomatoes | 西红柿 | potato | potatoes | 土豆，马铃薯 |
| mango | mangoes | 芒果 | zero | zeros | 零，零号 |

### 四、以 s，x，ch，sh 结尾的词名词变复数时，要在词尾加 es

| 单数 | 复数 | 词义 | 单数 | 复数 | 词义 |
| --- | --- | --- | --- | --- | --- |
| bus | buses | 公共汽车 | class | classes | 班级 |
| box | boxes | 盒子 | fox | foxes | 狐狸 |
| match | matches | 火柴，比赛 | lunch | lunches | 午餐 |
| brush | brushes | 画笔，刷子 | | | |

### 五、以 man 结尾表示一类人的，变 man 为 men

| 单数 | 复数 | 词义 | 单数 | 复数 | 词义 |
| --- | --- | --- | --- | --- | --- |
| man | men | 男人 | woman | women | 女人，妇女 |
| policeman | policemen | 警察 | fireman | firemen | 消防员 |

### 六、单复数同形的

| 单数 | 复数 | 词义 | 单数 | 复数 | 词义 |
| --- | --- | --- | --- | --- | --- |
| deer | deer | 鹿 | sheep | sheep | 绵羊 |
| fish | fish | 鱼 | Chinese | Chinese | 中国人 |
| Japanese | Japanese | 日本人 | works | works | 工厂 |

### 七、单词中有 oo 的，变 oo 为 ee

| 单数 | 复数 | 词义 | 单数 | 复数 | 词义 |
| --- | --- | --- | --- | --- | --- |
| foot | feet | 脚 | tooth | teeth | 牙齿 |
| goose | geese | 鹅 | | | |

**Finish the Blanks with Corresponding Forms.**

1. I have two _____. （knife）

2. There are many _____ here. （box）

3. There are many _____ on the road. （bus）

4. A few _____ are drawing on the wall.（boy）
5. The _____ are playing football now.（child）
6. Please take two _____ for me.（photo）
7. I like the red _____ .（tomato）
8. Would you please clean your _____ now?（tooth）
9. Do you want some _____?（milk）
10. There are ten _____ _____ in our school.（woman teacher）

# Part Ⅲ　Grammar Focus

## 被动语态（The Passive Voice）

### 一、定义

被动语态是动词的一种形式，用以说明主语与谓语动词之间的关系。英语的语态共有两种：主动语态和被动语态。主动语态表示主语是动作的执行者，被动语态表示主语是动作的承受者。

### 二、形式

1. 把主动态动词变成被动态，是把助动词 be 变为主动态动词原来的时态，再加上主要动词的过去分词，也就是构成 be done 的基本形式。主动态动词的主语这时变为被动态动词的施动者。这个施动者常常不被提到。若要提到，可置于 by 之后或放在从句的后面：

My grandfather planted <u>this tree</u>.　我爷爷种下了这棵树。（主动语态）
　　　　　　　　　　（宾语）

<u>This tree</u> was planted by my grandfather.　这棵树是（被）我爷爷种下的。
主语　　　　　　　　　　　　　　　　　　　　　　　　（被动语态）

2. 主动语态和被动语态的对比（以 do 为例）：

| 时态/动词形式 | 主动语态 | 被动语态 |
| --- | --- | --- |
| 一般现在时 | do/does | am/is/are done |
| 一般过去时 | did | was/were done |
| 一般将来时 | will do | will be done |
| 现在进行时 | am/is/are doing | am/is/are being done |
| 过去进行时 | was/were doing | was/were being done |
| 现在完成时 | have/has done | have/has been done |
| 过去完成时 | had done | had been done |
| 情态动词 | must/may/can do | must/may/can be done |

## Unit 4  Office Affairs

We keep the butter here. （主动语态）
The butter is kept here. （被动语态）

3. 各个进行时态的被动态要求用 be 的进行式加上主要动词的过去分词：

They are repairing the bridge. （主动语态）
The bridge is being repaired. （被动语态）

4. 情态动词的被动语态：在情态动词后加上 be 动词的原形，再加过去分词：

You should shut these doors. （主动语态）
These doors should be shut. （被动语态）

## Task 1  Multiple Choice.

**Directions：**Complete each one by deciding on the most appropriate word or words from the four choices.

1. English _____ in Britain.
   A. speaks          B. are spoken       C. is speaking      D. is spoken
2. This popular song _____ by us after class.
   A. often sings     B. often sang       C. is often sang    D. is often sung
3. This kind of bike _____ in Germany.
   A. makes           B. made             C. is making        D. is made
4. New computers _____ in our school.
   A. is used         B. are using        C. are used         D. have used
5. Our flat must _____ clean.
   A. keep            B. be kept          C. to be kept       D. to keep
6. A new hospital _____ at the corner of the street.
   A. is building     B. is being built   C. been built       D. be building
7. The key _____ on the sofa when I left.
   A. was left        B. will be left     C. is left          D. has been left
8. The sports meeting _____ be held until next week.
   A. didn't          B. won't            C. isn't            D. doesn't
9. These papers _____ yet.
   A. have not written              B. have not been written
   C. has not written               D. has not been written
10. French _____ in every country.
    A. is not spoken                 B. are spoken
    C. is speaking                   D. is not speaking

**Task 2　Finish the Blanks with Corresponding Forms.**

1. _____ this kind of car _____ ( produce ) in Shanghai?
2. The new production line can _____ ( put ) into use next month.
3. _____ the film _____ ( show ) many times since last Sunday?
4. Look, some new houses _____ ( build ) there.
5. The colour TV _____ ( buy ) in that shop three days ago.
6. The doctor said Jim must _____ ( operate ) on at once.
7. —_____ the bridge _____ ( repair ) yet?
   —Yes.
8. We are in Grade One this year, so we _____ ( teach ) physics next year.
9. —Where _____ ( be ) you last night?
   —I _____ ( ask ) to help Tom at home.
10. The Great Wall _____ ( know ) all over the world.

**Task 3　Rewrite the Following Sentences with Passive Voice.**

1. Mr. Smith told us some customs of England.
   We _____ _____ some customs of England.
2. You can keep the book for two weeks.
   The book can _____ _____ for two weeks.
3. The recent tsunami killed over 140,000 people.
   Over 140,000 people _____ _____ by the recent tsunami.
4. We should take good care of our desks.
   Our desks should _____ _____ good care of.
5. Many students are cleaning the classroom.
   The classroom _____ _____ _____ by many students.
6. They saw a UFO flying in the sky.
   A UFO _____ _____ flying in the sky.
7. I haven't finished my homework yet.
   My homework _____ _____ _____ yet.
8. We will hold the meeting this afternoon.
   The meeting will _____ _____ this afternoon.
9. The writer gave her a book after talking to her.
   A book _____ _____ to her by the writer after he talked to her.
10. Did he repair this desk yesterday?
    _____ this desk _____ yesterday?

## Part Ⅳ  Text 2

### Preview Questions

**Work in pairs and discuss the following questions.**
1. What are the difficulties for people working from home?
2. Which is more efficient, working from home or working in the office?
3. How can you improve efficiency of working from home?

**Background Information**

Since more and more people are required to work from home during the pandemic, many of them are worrying about their efficiency. Because it is their first time and there are a lot of distractions when working at home. So how can you be productive when working from home? The following article provides you with some tips.

## How to Work from Home during the Coronavirus Outbreak[①]

Working from home is not a new concept. However, it has become more popular now that COVID-19 has taken over our lives. More and more people are now choosing to work from home to keep themselves, and others safe. Many of them do not have a choice as their employers insist on them working from home.

You might have to change the way you work almost entirely, but your work will be the same, so there really isn't much to worry about. Let us discuss how you can effectively work from home during these trying times.

Creating a schedule is the most important. Make sure that you know when to work and when to take breaks. Make sure that your children are comfortably set in an environment where they are so busy that they do not interfere with your work.

Choosing a peaceful environment is necessary to your success in working from home. Choose a room that is away from the rest of the house and consider it as your office.

Bring your critical gear with you. Depending on the nature of your work, make sure that you have your pencils, pens, paper, notebooks, and whatever else you need with you.

Communicating more often than you usually do is vital when you have just begun to work from home. Since many things will be confusing for you, and other people who you work with, it is important that you talk to them more often. Using tools such as Hangouts Meet, and Zoom and other similar applications will help you stay in touch with your coworkers, supervisors,

---

① 本文改编自网站 cover letters and resume, 时间 2020.11.1, 原网址: https://coverlettersandresume.com/articles

and subordinates.

Technology plays a dynamic role in your success in working from home. A good Internet connection and a fast computer will help you meet your deadlines more efficiently. You need to remember that many people will be using technology to while away their time, as they are locked up inside during the pandemic. Internet may be slow-a backup Internet connection should be arranged so that your work isn't affected.

**New Words**

concept/'kɑnsɛpt/ n. 概念；观念；想法
schedule/'skɛdʒul/ vt. 安排 n. 时间表
*gear/gɪr/ n. 设备
*vital/'vaɪtl/ adj. 极重要的；必不可少的
confusing/kən'fju:zɪŋ/ adj. 莫名其妙的；难以理解的
application/[ˌæplɪ'keɪʃn]/ n. 申请；应用
*supervisor/'supərˌvaɪzər/ n. 监督者；管理者
*subordinate/[sə'bɔːdɪnət]/ adj. 下级的；次要的
deadline/'dɛdlaɪn/ n. 截止期限
affect/ə'fɛkt/ vt. 影响；感染

**Phrases and Expressions**

take over    接管
insist on    坚决要求
interfere with    干扰；妨碍
stay in touch with    与……保持联络
play a role in    在……发挥作用
lock up    关起来；锁定

**Proper Nouns**

Hangouts Meet    环聊（谷歌公司一款视频群聊系统）
Zoom    一款多人手机云视频会议软件

**Notes**

1. However, it has become more popular now that COVID-19 has taken over our lives. 本句说COVID-19接管（take over）了我们的生活，指的是疫情在很大程度上影响着我们的生活。

2. It is important that you talk to them more often. 这里属于虚拟语气用法，"It is+ 形容词 +that"句型当中，从句当中的动词需要使用"should+ 动词原形"，其中should可以省略，如"It is necessary that（should）she talk to you first."。

3. You need to remember that many people will be using technology to while away their time, as they are locked up inside during the pandemic. 其中 as 表示"因为"，相当于 because，"they are locked up"为本单元所讲被动用法，指的是疫情期间人们在家隔离。"will be using"为将来进行时的用法，指的是将来时间点或某个时间段正在进行的动作。如"I will be travelling in Thailand next week."。

## Multiple-Choice Questions

Choose the best answer for each of the following questions or statements according to the text.

1. Which is the most important when working from home?
    A. Schedule
    B. Network
    C. Communication
    D. Equipment
2. Which is not the reason for employees to choose working from home?
    A. Because they want to keep themselves safe
    B. Because they want to keep others safe
    C. Because their employers require them to work from home
    D. Because they want to improve their work efficiency
3. How can you avoid the interference of your kids when working from home?
    A. By buying them food
    B. By letting them play games
    C. By keeping them busy in a comfortable environment
    D. By asking them to study
4. Why is the Internet slow during the pandemic?
    A. Because there are no people to maintain the network
    B. Because there are many people using the Internet
    C. Because people can't afford good Internet
    D. Because your computer is not good enough

# Part Ⅴ  Exercises

## Task 1  Vocabulary and Structure.

### Section A  Multiple Choice.

Directions: Complete each one by deciding on the most appropriate word or words from the four choices.

1. Her every waking hour _____ by work.

  A. is occupied    B. occupy

  C. occupied    D. are occupied

2. His bad behaviour _____ his expulsion（开除）from school.

  A. result of   B. result to   C. result in   D. result for

3. You should always focus _____ quality, not quantity.

  A. at   B. to   C. on   D. with

4. I have no _____ reasons to refuse your invitation.

  A. communicating    B. computing

  C. commuting    D. compelling

5. They increased profits by cutting _____ the cost.

  A. up   B. down   C. off   D. in

6. What he said is _____ so that I can't understand.

  A. confuse   B. confused   C. confusing   D. confusion

7. Many people _____ in their house because of the COVID-19.

  A. lock up    B. is locked up

  C. was locked up    D. were locked up

8. He was deeply _____ by my words.

  A. affect   B. affected   C. effected   D. effort

9. The firm was taken _____ by an international company.

  A. over   B. out   C. on   D. off

10. I can't go because I have to meet the _____.

  A. deadline   B. deadlock   C. deadly   D. deadhead

**Section B Blank Filling.**

11. His job _____ (apply) was rejected by the company.

12. The students felt _____ (inspire) by the teacher's words.

13. Many workers are yearning _____ (go) back to office.

14. Most people use video games for _____ (entertain).

15. In some cases, employees _____ (require) to stay at home by their employers.

## Task 2 Translation.

  Directions: This part, numbered 1 through 5, is to test your ability to translate English into Chinese. Each of the four sentences (No. 1 to No. 4) is followed by four choices of suggested translation marked A, B, C, and D. Mark the best choice and circle the corresponding letter. Write your translation of the paragraph (No.5) in the corresponding space.

1. Her illness was a result of overwork.

Unit 4　Office Affairs

   A. 她因为生病导致没有去工作。
   B. 她生病了无法过度工作。
   C. 她生病是因过度工作引起的。
   D. 她的病带来的结果就是过度工作。
2. The productivity can be increased in a comfy working environment.
   A. 生产力能够提高工作环境的舒适度。
   B. 舒适的工作环境能够提高生产力。
   C. 舒适的工作环境能提高产品数量。
   D. 产品能够被舒适的工作环境提高。
3. This information will be less confusing if it's produced in the form of table.
   A. 如果将这个信息放在桌子里,它将减少疑惑。
   B. 如果将这个信息制成表格形式,它将减少疑惑。
   C. 如果这个信息是以表格的形式制作的,它将不会那么令人疑惑。
   D. 如果这个信息被生产后放在桌子里,这一信息将不会令人疑惑。
4. Employees are never allowed to let their personal feelings to interfere with their work.
   A. 员工从不让他们的私人感情影响工作。
   B. 员工不被允许让其私人感情妨碍工作。
   C. 个人感情不应该被员工带入工作中。
   D. 雇员不允许他们的感觉影响工作。
5. You see your coworkers for eight, ten or even twelve hours in a day, sharing personal details, work space and even assignments. They can make work more (or less) enjoyable depending on how good your relationship is. A poor relationship can lead to poor productivity while a healthy relationship can lead to personal growth and a positive work environment. However, building relationships requires both work and respect not just on your part but on the part of your coworker as well.

_____
_____
_____
_____
_____
_____
_____

# Part VI  Writing: Memo（备忘录）

## A. 什么是备忘录?

Memo is a written massage sent by one person to another or a group of people within the same organization. This internal communication can be from superior to subordinate, e.g. from Managing Director to Sales Manager, or the other way around; it can also go between equals.

## B. 备忘录的格式:

Title Heading: Memorandum

To: recipients' names and job titles

From: your name and job title

Date: current date

Subject: The subject line should be specific enough to convey the main purpose of the memo. For example: "Employee Benefits Meeting".

Body: including opening, discussing and closing segment.

## C. Sample:

### Memo

To: Divisional Personnel Managers

From: The Managing Director

Date: Jan 18, 2021

Subject: Coffee-Making Facilities

There have been a number of comments on the amount of coffee consumed in the company. I do not want to sound as though I am against coffee-drinking. Actually, coffee plays a dynamic role in increasing productivity. And I believe time-saving machines for making tea and coffee do exist.

We never know how the officer will react if we are not careful. In any case, we are thinking of putting in tea and coffee machines. Please send me a report.

## Task 1  Fill in the blanks based on the information given below.

说明：假定你是销售部经理 John Green，请给本公司其他各部门经理写一个内部通知。通知时间为 2020 年 6 月 16 日，通知主题为讨论 2020 年第三季度（the 3rd quarter）销售计划。

内容：本部门已制订 2020 年第三季度销售计划。于 2020 年 6 月 19 日下午 1:00 在本公司会议室开会讨论这一计划，希望各部门经理前来参会。如不能到会，请提前告知本部门秘书。

To: 1_____
From: John Green, Sales Manger
Date: June 16th, 2020
2_____: Discuss the sales plan for the 3rd quarter of 2020

  Our Department has made the 3 _____ for the 3rd quarter of 2020. To discuss the plan, a meeting will be held in the 4_____ of our corporation at 1:00 p.m. on June 19th, 2020.

  Managers of all the departments are required to attend the meeting. If anyone cannot be present, please notify the 5_____ of the Sales Department in advance.

## Task 2　Practical writing: Write a memo based on the information given below.

  假如今天是 2021 年 1 月 10 日，你是公司总经理 Jason White，请给董事会全体成员发一份备忘录，主要内容如下：本公司将于 1 月 20 日上午 9 点在本公司会议室讨论下一季度销售计划，请务必按时到会，如有其他安排无法到会，请提前告知秘书。

# Unit 5  Internet

> **Goals**
> In this unit, we will learn to:
> 1. talk about the advantages and disadvantages of the Internet;
> 2. have a good command of English expressions about the Internet;
> 3. get familiar with different Internet-related topics;
> 4. write an E-mail.

## Part I  Listening & Speaking

**Task 1  Look and Say: Look at the following pictures and choose the right letters (A—F) to match the pictures below.**

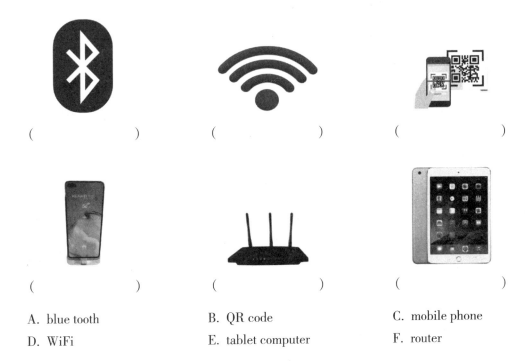

(　　)　　　(　　)　　　(　　)

(　　)　　　(　　)　　　(　　)

A. blue tooth　　　B. QR code　　　C. mobile phone
D. WiFi　　　　　 E. tablet computer　F. router

Task 2　Listen and answer: You will hear two conversations. After each conversation, you will hear some questions. Choose the best answer to each question.

**Conversation 1**

1. A. Build a website　　　　　　　　B. Design a website
   C. Open a shop　　　　　　　　　D. Browse website
2. A. Easy　　　　　　　　　　　　B. Difficult
   C. Interested　　　　　　　　　　D. Excited
3. A. It is the best program the woman has used.
   B. It is a popular program for website building.
   C. The man doesn't know about the program at all.
   D. The woman is learning program from her friend.

**Conversation 2**

4. A. Booking tickets　　　　　　　　B. Shopping online
   C. Watching Videos　　　　　　　D. Building a website
5. A. The line of booking tickets is always busy.
   B. He lost his money.
   C. His mobile phone was out of work.
   D. The tickets have been sold out.
6. A. Order the tickets directly from the counter.
   B. Order the tickets through the Internet.
   C. Order the tickets through the telephone.
   D. Order the tickets through his friends.

Task 3　Listen and Fill: Listen to the dialogue below twice and fill in the blanks. After listening, read the dialogue carefully and act it out with your partner.

　　　Lily moved out of her dorm room and moved into a new apartment. She is now talking to her friend Jack about the Internet connection. Fill in the missing information based on what you hear.
Jack: Hey, Lily, have you finished moving out of your dorm room yet?
Lily: Yeah, I've all done. I moved into my 1_____ _____ off-campus yesterday.
Jack: 2_____ _____ _____ _____ _____ ?
Lily: It's great. There's just one problem.

Jack: What's that?

Lily: Well, I don't have 3 _____ _____ _____ in my new apartment so I can't use the computer to 4 _____ _____ _____ from my room.

Jack: And that's really important.

Lily: Right. I need it to do research for classes, 5 _____ _____, stuff like that. I use it almost every day.

Jack: So are you going to pay to 6 _____ _____ _____ in the apartment?

Lily: Well, I've called a couple of 7 _____ _____ in the area and it's no trouble for them to send someone out to my apartment to install 8 _____ _____. It's just the cost. I have to pay every month for the service.

Jack: Well, you know, there's always a computer center on campus. The computers there have 9 _____ _____ _____. Couldn't you use them?

Lily: I could. It's just that I don't have classes every day, so I'd have to go campus on some days just to use the Internet. And that computer center can 10 _____ _____ sometimes.

Jack: Mmm.

Lily: So, I'm not sure what to do.

## Task 4  Discuss and Debate: The Internet, is it a chance or a threat?

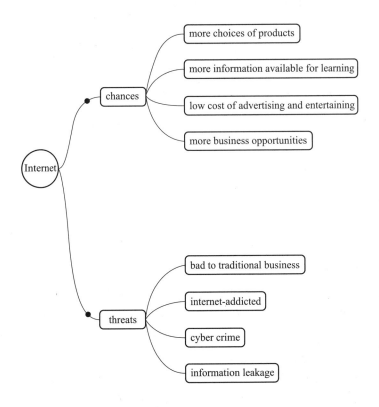

# Part Ⅱ  Text 1

## Preview Questions

**Work in pairs and discuss the following questions.**

1. What will you do on the Internet if you are bored?
2. Why do people use the Internet?
3. What are the advantages and disadvantage of the Internet?

## Background Information

Since its arrival, the Internet has changed many aspects of our lives. It has dramatically changed how people learn, shop, work, communicate, have fun, socialize, and read about current affairs. Today we will tell you about the fun things you can do on the Internet if you are bored and need to kill time.

## Fun Things to Do on the Internet[①]

The Internet is an inexhaustible source of fun and entertainment. Here you can work, create, play, sell and buy everything, make friends, and even find love.

**Watch videos, TV programs, and movies**

The Internet is a great platform for short videos and experimental movies. Here you can find millions of clips, funny videos, and breath-catching short films. The most popular source is surely YouTube, where people upload millions of videos every day.

On this platform, you can study, learn how to do things yourself, and find any information you need. Another useful resource is TED Talks, which contains short lectures on a variety of subjects including education, technology, and relationships.

**Listen to radio programs**

Many radio stations keep records of their past programs and eagerly post them online. For example, on National Public Radio or Public Radio International, you may find classical programs, listen to charts, and use a convenient search <u>option</u> to find the stories you are interested in.

**Sell the things you don't need**

You probably know that it is possible to sell everything no matter how unusual or useless this object seems. When having some free time, head to eBay or a similar website to find out

---

① 本文改编自 Market Business News 5/21/2020；作者 Edward Bishop；原文网址 https://marketbusinessnews.com/things-do-on-the-Internet/235251/

what your things are worth.

Just create a free eBay account (if you still don't have one), choose the advanced search, and insert keywords about the item you are willing to sell. When pressing the search bar, you'll see similar items and their price. Then create an ad with photos and descriptions of your good, and you will earn some money.

**Learn any course and languages**

There is a great number of reliable websites, where you can learn different courses, gain new skills, and even get a degree. Pick one of the hundreds of categories, subscribe for a free or paid mode, and join thousands of other students in a virtual classroom.

**Explore the Earth**

Google Earth is a downloadable program, which allows flying around our beautiful planet and zooming interesting places. When getting close to the ground, you'll see pictures made by regular users and Wikipedia links.

**The time spent with use**

Sometimes we are so tired from work and studies that we don't feel like doing anything. The best decision is to let your mind relax and to go online visiting useless websites or playing simple games.

However, the Internet is not only about killing time and it may be rather useful: learn something new, read books, watch programs, sell things, and even make a tour to space. It's only up to you to decide what your Internet journey will look like today.

**New Words**

  *inexhaustible/ˌɪnɪɡˈzɔːstəbl/ adj. 用之不竭的；无穷无尽的
  entertainment/ˌentəˈteɪnmənt/ n. 娱乐活动；招待；款待
  platform/ˈplætfɔːm/ n. 平台；站台
  *experimental/ɪkˌsperɪˈmentl/ adj. 实验性的；科学实验的
  clip/klɪp/ n. 片段；回形针；剪短；修剪
  upload/ˌʌpˈləʊd/ v. 上载；上传
  classical/ˈklæsɪkl/ adj. 古典的；经典的；传统的
  chart/tʃɑːt/ n. 图表；每周流行唱片排行榜
  convenient/kənˈviːniənt/ adj. 实用的；便利的；省事的
  description/dɪˈskrɪpʃn/ n. 描写（文字）；形容；说明
  *category/ˈkætəɡəri/ n. （人或事物的）类别，种类
  *subscribe/səbˈskraɪb/ v. 定期订购（或订阅等）；定期交纳（会员费）
  *virtual/ˈvɜːtʃuəl/ adj. 很接近的；实际上的；虚拟的
  *zoom/zuːm/ v. 快速移动；急剧增长

**Phrases and Expressions**

  millions of 数百万

  a variety of 种种；各种各样的……

  keep records of 把……记录下来；保持……的记录

  be willing to 愿意

  a great number of 许多

  advanced research 高级检索

  search bar 搜索条；搜索栏

  feel like 想要做……

**Proper Nouns**

  YouTube 优兔；一个视频网站

  TED（=Technology, Entertainment, Design）一个国际会议机构，它是技术、娱乐、设计的缩写。TED 是美国的一家私有非营利机构，该机构以它组织的 TED 大会著称。

  TED Talks TED 演讲

  National Public Radio 美国国家公共电台

  Public Radio International 国际公共广播电台

  eBay 易贝

  Google Earth 谷歌地球

**Notes**

  1. YouTube 是一个视频网站，由美籍华人陈士骏等人创立，让用户下载、观看及分享影片或短片。

  2. You probably know that it is possible to sell everything no matter how unusual or useless this object seems. 您可能知道，无论物品看起来多么与众不同或无用，都有可能卖得出去。"it is possible to sell…"表示"卖……是可能的"。it 为形式主语，真正的主语是后面的动词不定式短语。"no matter"是"无论"的意思，引导让步状语从句。

  3. eBay 即"易贝"，是一个管理可让全球民众上网买卖物品的线上拍卖及购物网站。

  4. There is a great number of reliable websites, where you can learn different courses, gain new skills, and even get a degree. 互联网上有大量可靠的网站，您可以学习不同的课程、获得新技能甚至获得学位。"a great number of"表示"许多的，大量的"，后面接复数名词，相当于"a great many, a lot of 或 lots of"。where 引导定语从句时，其作为关系副词，此时，where 可以转换成"介词+which"的结构。

  5. Google Earth 即谷歌地球，是一款虚拟地球仪软件，由 Google 公司于 2005 年 6 月正式推出。它把卫星照片、航空照相和 GIS 布置在一个地球的三维模型上。

Unit 5　Internet

## Task 1　Answer the following questions according to the text.

1. What is the Internet according to the text?

2. What can you do on National Public Radio or Public Radio International?

3. What is Google Earth according to the text?

4. What is the best decision when sometimes we are so tired from work and studies that we don't feel like doing anything?

5. Is the Internet just killing time? Why?

## Task 2　Choose the best answer for each of the following questions or statements according to the text.

1. What is the most popular platform for short videos?
   A. Hulu
   B. You Tube
   C. Showtime
   D. Metacafe
2. According to the article, what type of video can be found on TED?
   A. Online music platform
   B. Shopping platform online
   C. Short lectures on a variety of subjects
   D. Online movie App
3. What is the meaning of the underlined word in "You may find classical programs, listen to charts, and use a convenient search option to find the stories you are interested in"?
   A. guide
   B. point
   C. bar
   D. choice
4. Which of the following is not a function of the Internet?
   A. To see a doctor
   B. To learn any course and languages
   C. To listen to radio programs
   D. To watch videos, TV programs and movies
5. What is the text mainly talking about?
   A. Fun things to do on the Internet
   B. Listening to radio programs on the Internet

C. Learning any course and languages on the Internet
D. Selling the things you don't need on the Internet

## Task 3　常见形容词和副词后缀（Common Suffixes of Adjectives and Adverbs）

| 后缀 | 意义 | 举例 |
| --- | --- | --- |
| -ful，-less | -ful 表示"充满……的"含义；-less 表示否定"无……的" | careful, useful, careless, useless |
| -able，-ible | "能……的""可以（被）……的""具有……特点的" | reasonable, acceptable, responsible, horrible |
| -al | "属于……的""有……特性的" | personal, national, arrival, exceptional |
| -ent，-ant | "……性的" | different, excellent, important, distant |
| -ous | 表法"充满……的""具有……特征的" | dangerous, continuous |
| -ly（adj.）-ly（adv.） | "像……的""有……性质的""每……的"；如是形容词之后加"-ly"则构成副词 | friendly（adj.），brotherly（adj.）；hourly（adj.），daily（adj.），happily（adv.）firstly（adv.） |
| -y | 表示"多……的""有……的""如……的" | rainy, smoky, silvery, sleepy |

According to the word formation above, please match the suffixes in column A with the words in column B.

| Column A | Column B | Column A | Column B |
| --- | --- | --- | --- |
| 1. -ful | A. suit | 6. -ant | F. patience |
| 2. -less | B. home | 7. -al | G. sense |
| 3. -able | C. hope | 8. -y | H. man |
| 4. -ible | D. nature | 9. -ous | I. noise |
| 5. -ent | E. instance | 10. -ly（adj） | J. desire |

## Part Ⅲ　Grammar Focus

### 形容词和副词（Adjectives & Adverbs）

#### 一、定义和用法

| 种类 | 意义 | 定语 | 表语 | 宾补 | 状语 |
| --- | --- | --- | --- | --- | --- |
| 形容词（adj.） | 形容词用于修饰名词或代词，表示人或事物的属性或特征等 | √ | √ | √ | √ |
| 副词（adv.） | 副词是用来说明动作或状态的特征，说明时间、地点、程度等概念。它用来修饰动词、形容词、副词、短语或句子 | √ | √ | √ | √ |

　　1. 多个形容词排序：指示代词（物主代词，冠词）+ 数词 + 描绘性形容词 + 大小长短高低 + 新旧 + 颜色 + 国籍 + 材料 + 用途 + 名词，如"these two big grey British castles"。

　　2. 副词分类：时间副词（now, then, soon, early, ago），频度副词（usually, never, sometimes），地点副词（here, home, near, above），方式副词（quickly, hard, suddenly），程度副词（much, almost, very, hardly），疑问副词（when, where, how, why），关系副词（when, where, why），连接副词（why, how, if, whether, when）。

#### 二、形容词和副词等级（Adjective & Adverb Degrees）

　　比较的等级分为三类：原级（Positive degree），比较级（Comparative Degree）和最高级（Superlative Degree）。

　　1. 原级。

　　（1）同级比较的肯定形式：as+ 原级 +as（和……一样）。

　　（2）同级比较的否定形式：not so（as）+ 原级 +as（和……不一样）。

　　（3）表示"几倍于……"用"倍数 +as+ 形容词 +as"。

　　2. 比较级。

　　（1）两个事物比较，表示一个比另一个"更……"，用"比较级 +than"的结构。

　　（2）用"the+ 比较级，the+ 比较级"的结构表示"越……，越……"的意思。

　　（3）表示持续不断变化的可以用"比较级 +and+ 比较级"的结构，意为"越来越"。

　　（4）形容词和副词的比较级前可用 much, far, a lot, a little, a bit 等词与词组来修饰，表示"……得多""稍微……"等意义。

　　3. 最高级。

　　（1）三个和三个以上的事物比较用"the+ 最高级"结构，表示"最"的意思。

（2）有时最高级表示"非常"和"很"的意思，这时可以加不定冠词 a/an 或不加冠词。

## Task 1  Write down the comparative and superlative degrees of the following adjectives and adverbs.

1. big         (          ) (          )    2. good         (          ) (          )
3. long        (          ) (          )    4. wide         (          ) (          )
5. little      (          ) (          )    6. beautiful    (          ) (          )
7. far         (          ) (          )    8. bad          (          ) (          )
9. early       (          ) (          )   10. quickly      (          ) (          )

## Task 2  Correct the mistakes in the sentences：

1. This box is more heavier than that one.
2. Tom is the youngest in the three.
3. He is taller of the two.
4. Today is our the busiest day.
5. I think math is very more difficult than Chinese.
6. There are much more people in the street than usual.
7. Mike is so tall as Jack.
8. Li Ying jumped farther than Jim jumped.
9. The Yellow River is the second longer river in China.
10. We must get farther information.

## Task 3  Put the right forms in the brackets.

1. Mobile phones are not as_____（expensive）as before.
2. Gas prices are_____（low）here than in other parts of the country.
3. The novel turned out to be_____（successful）than he had expected.
4. Some people think_____（much）about their duties than their rights.
5. This task is_____（difficult）than the one I have finished.
6. Lightning is seen before thunder（雷）is heard，because light travels_____（fast）than sound.
7. The harder you work，the_____（well）you will be able to finish the task.
8. Computers are very popular now and they are_____（cheap）than before.
9. Of all the books in this shop，this one is the_____（good）.
10. Tom is the_____（clever）student I have ever seen.

## Part Ⅳ　Text 2

### Preview Questions

**Work in pairs and discuss the following questions.**
1. What is 5G?
2. When will 5G be available?
3. What can 5G do?

**Background Information**

　　In 2019, a big technology shift will finally begin. It's a once-in-a-decade upgrade to our wireless systems that will start reaching mobile phone users. The transition to new fifth—generation cellular networks—known as 5G for short. This new era will leap ahead of current wireless technology, known as 4G, by offering mobile Internet speeds that will let people download entire movies within seconds and most likely bring big changes to video games, sports and shopping.

---

　　There has been a lot of reports recently about 5G, the next generation of wireless technology for the world. But what is this technology and how might it change our lives?

### What is 5G?

　　5G stands for fifth generation, meaning the next step in the progression of technology to replace the current 4G system. 4G was the replacement for 3G, which came after 2G, and so on. These systems are wireless computer networks.

　　Earlier "G" systems were designed to improve mobile communication operations. Each new technology brought major improvements in speed and greatly increased network capacity.

　　The new 5G system promises more of the same. It is expected to permit more users to do more things at a faster rate[①]. Higher Internet speeds and larger network capacity should result in better performance for device users connected to 5G.

However, technology experts say there is a major way that 5G is different from the earlier systems. It will move well beyond mobile network technology to affect many more devices and industries than other "G" versions.

### When will it be available?

Before we can all use 5G, wireless companies and phone makers will have to complete and deploy a whole new system. New phones and communication equipment must be built.

American wireless companies have been preparing for the new system for some time. They have been creating new network equipment and buying broadcasting space to carry 5G signals. They have built new 5G antennas to serve American cities and towns. Wireless providers will invest at least $275 billion in 5G-related networks in the United States, the industry group CTIA reported.

The first U.S. launch of 5G is expected to happen sometime this year. Industry experts expect it will take a few more years to go nationwide. It will take even longer to reach rural areas.

China is expected to launch 5G sometime in 2020, while European nations are likely to build their systems more slowly over time.

In the United States, the first 5G-ready phones should be available in the first half of this year. The first 5G iPhone, however, is not expected until 2020. 4G phones will work on 5G networks, but not at 5G speeds.

### What can 5G do?

Wireless industry groups say 5G will help fuel future "smart cities" by connecting sensor networks. Such networks will be able to control vehicle traffic and quickly identify streetlight outages.

5G is also expected to connect self-driving cars and support new technologies involving virtual reality. Higher 5G speeds could also permit doctors to commonly perform remote medical operations. Factories and businesses could use 5G technology to increase automation and improve the collection of information.

### New Words

wireless/ˈwaɪələs/  adj. 无线的

generation/ˌdʒenəˈreɪʃn/  n. 一代人，同辈人；代，一代

*progression/prəˈɡreʃn/  n. 进程；系列；序列

---

① 本文摘自可可英语 VOA 慢速 – 科技报道 2/14/2019 原文网址：http://3g.kekenet.com/broadcast/201902/578531.shtml

replace/rɪˈpleɪs/   v. 取代；代替
improvement/ɪmˈpruːvmənt/   n. 改进；改善
*capacity/kəˈpæsəti/   n. 容量；职责
device/dɪˈvaɪs/   n. 装置；设备；仪器；器具
*deploy/dɪˈplɔɪ/   v. 部署；有效地利用；调动
signal/ˈsɪgnəl/   n. 信号；标志
*antenna/ænˈtenə/   n. 天线
*nationwide/ˌneɪʃnˈwaɪd/   adj. 在全国范围内；就全国而论
rural/ˈrʊərəl/   adj. 农村的；乡村的；似农村的
sensor/ˈsensə(r)/   n. 传感器，探测设备
*identify/aɪˈdentɪfaɪ/   v. 鉴定；确认；发现；认出
outage/ˈaʊtɪdʒ/   n. 停电（等）期间
*automation/ˌɔːtəˈmeɪʃn/   n. 自动化

**Phrases and Expressions**

stand for    代表；代替；象征
and so on    诸如此类；等等
result in    导致；引起；造成
prepare for    为……做准备；筹备
at least    至少；不少于

**Proper Nouns**

CTIA    美国无线通信和互联网协会

**Notes**

1. It is expected to permit more users to do more things at a faster rate. 预计 5G 将允许更多用户以更快的速度处理更多事情。It is expected to ...（预计……），permit sb. to do sth.（允许某人做某事），at a faster rate（以更快的速度）。

2. However, technology experts say there is a major way that 5G is different from the earlier systems. 但是，技术专家表示，5G 与此前的系统存在一个主要的不同之处。这个句子中包含两个从句，其中 say 引导宾语从句，省略引导词 that，a major way that... 引导定语从句。

3. American wireless companies have been preparing for the new system for some time. 一段时间以来，美国无线运营商一直在为新系统做准备。"have been preparing for" 表示"一直在为……做准备"，属于现在完成进行时。

4. Industry experts expect it will take a few more years to go nationwide. 行业专家预计，5G 网络需要数年的时间才能在全美范围内推广。go 用作连系动词时，通常表示主语处于某种状态或由某种状态向另一种状态转变，后面多接形容词作其表语。

5. 5G is also expected to connect self-driving cars and support new technologies involving virtual reality. 5G 还将连接自动驾驶车辆并支持与虚拟现实有关的新技术。involving 表示"涉及，谈到，有关"，virtual reality 即虚拟现实。

## Multiple-Choice Questions

**Choose the best answer for each of the following questions or statements according to the text.**

1. What is the next step in the progression of technology to replace the current 4G system?
   A. 2G            B. 3G            C. 5G            D. 6G
2. Earlier "G" systems were designed to_____.
   A. Improve mobile communication operations
   B. Improve communication operations
   C. Improve mobile communication
   D. Improve mobile communication network
3. According to the report of CTIA, how much will wireless providers invest in 5G-related networks in the United States?
   A. At least $75 million            B. $275 billion
   C. At least $275 billion           D. $275 million
4. How will 5G help fuel future "smart cities"?
   A. By connecting sensor networks to control vehicle traffic and quickly identify streetlight outages.
   B. By enabling doctors to commonly perform remote medical operations.
   C. By enabling factories to increase automation and improve the collection of information.
   D. All above.
5. What is the best title for this text?
   A. Preparation Before 5G            B. 5G Functions
   C. What Is 5G Wireless Technology?  D. Is 5G Available Now?

# Part V  Exercises

## Task 1  Vocabulary and Structure.

**Section A   Multiple Choice.**

**Directions: Complete each one by deciding on the most appropriate word or words from the four choices.**

1. Our sales manager _____ deliver a speech at tomorrow's meeting.

|  | A. is expected to | B. was expected to |
|---|---|---|
|  | C. expected to | D. expects to |

2. He is likely _____ the job offers as he has some work experience in this line.

   A. getting  B. get  C. to get  D. got

3. If he were you, he _____ the company's website for more detailed information.

   A. would visit   B. will visit
   C. visit         D. have visited

4. They had an idea _____ they should invest in the Internet-related business.

   A. what   B. where   C. that   D. as

5. This hotel regard customer complaints as an opportunity to _____ its service.

   A. bring   B. receive   C. improve   D. obtain

6. He gave us a detailed _____ of the new proposal of his company.

   A. impression   B. explanation
   C. description   D. communication

7. He didn't feel like _____ to study.

   A. go   B. going   C. to go   D. gone

8. Smoking too much will _____ sickness.

   A. result in   B. result from   C. as a result   D. result on

9. The new style of dress is very popular and it is _____ in all sizes.

   A. important   B. active   C. available   D. famous

10. It is quite difficult for me _____ where to go.

    A. decide         B. having decided
    C. decide         D. to decide

## Section B  Blank Filling.

Directions: There are five incomplete statements here. You should fill in the blanks with the proper forms of the words given in the brackets.

11. The new bookcase at the exhibition _____ (design) by a Japanese company.

12. John has made the _____ (decide) to buy a new book on the Internet.

13. Modern means of _____ (communicate) can enable more people to work from home.

14. The new 5G system has _____ (great) increased network capacity.

15. Now the number of students who are learning on the Internet _____ (be) very large.

## Task 2  Translation.

Directions: This part, numbered 1 through 5, is to test your ability to translate English into Chinese. Each of the four sentences (No. 1 to No. 4) is followed by four choices of suggested translation marked A, B, C and D. Mark the best choice and circle the corresponding letter. Write your translation of the paragraph (No. 5) in the corresponding space.

1. I will give you a clear idea of the Internet in the region as soon as possible.
   A. 我会尽快让你们清楚地了解该地区的网络情况。
   B. 我将尽可能设法弄清楚该地区的网络情况。
   C. 我会尽早向你们清楚地说明该地区的网络状况。
   D. 我将尽可能对该地区网络状况提出明确的想法。

2. First of all, our purpose is to apply the Internet and technology to the solution of practical problems.
   A. 首先,提供解决实际问题的网络技术是我们的目标。
   B. 首先,我们的目的是运用网络技术来解决实际问题。
   C. 首先,我们的目标是在解决实际问题中依靠网络技术。
   D. 首先,我们申请网络项目的目的是解决实际问题。

3. 5G has played an important role in helping the doctors to perform remote medical operations.
   A. 5G 在帮助医生可以进行远程医疗手术方面发挥出了重要作用。
   B. 5G 能帮助医生进行远程医疗手术,并可以做出重大的贡献。
   C. 5G 对医生进行远程医疗手术的帮助是巨大的,并为他们的发展提供了平台。
   D. 5G 在帮助医生可以进行远程医疗手术中扮演了一个重要的角色。

4. Learning how to use the Internet effectively as a marketing tools means that you need to learn two different but related bodies of knowledge.
   A. 为了学习互联网这一营销工具手段,你需要学习两种不相关联的知识。
   B. 学习有效使用互联网和营销工具,你得学习互相关联但却各不相同的两大块知识。
   C. 如果你学会了这两大块不关联的知识,就等于学会了有效地在互联网上搞推销的工具。
   D. 学习有效地利用互联网作为营销工具,就意味着要学会两类互不相同却又互相关联的知识。

5. The way we buy has been revolutionized by the Internet. While online shopping saves a huge amount of your time, it also has its own drawbacks like poor quality sales, higher delivery charges and so on. If you are someone who loves the speed and easiness of online shopping, but you don't want to spend a fortune on your favourite dress or accessories, then this post is for you.

## Part Ⅵ　Writing: E-mails（电子邮件）

电子邮件是一种廉价快速的网络通信方式，可以是文字、图像、声音等多种形式。一般来说，电子邮件由两大部分组成。第一部分包括邮件地址（发件人，收件人）、日期、主题和附件；第二部分包括称呼、正文、结尾敬语和署名。

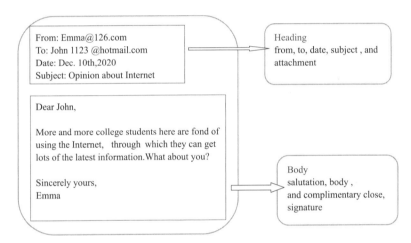

The components of an E-mail:

（1）Address——地址。

To：收信人地址　　　　From：寄件人地址

Cc：抄送收信人地址　　Bcc：密送收信人地址

If there is more than one address, half-width comma or semi-colon can be used to separate them.

（2）Subject（主题）。

① In subject, the general idea of this E-mail should be concise and clear to understand. Sometimes it can just be a word, such as greetings. A noun phrase or a sentence can also be served as a subject, but it should not be too long.

　　e.g. NO: News about the meeting　　YES: Tomorrow's meeting canceled

② Only the first letter in the first word or some proper nouns must be capitalized in subject.

③ You can also put "URGENT" or "FYI" (For Your Information) at the beginning of the subject.

　　e.g. URGENT: Submit your report today!

（3）Salutation（称呼）。

Salutation should flush with the left margin. Then put a comma or colon after that.

e.g. Dear Sir/Madam,

(4) Body—正文现代的齐头式(The Modern Blocked Form)。

In this format, salutation, complimentary close, signature and all paragraphs flush with the left margin. Paragraphs are doubled spaced and all line text single spaced.

(5) Ending(结尾)。

① To show great support to the cooperation and expectation.

e.g. We ensure our earnest and continued support.

② To make the address raise questions if he/she has any doubts.

e.g. Any question, please don't hesitate to let me know.

Please let me know if you have any question on this.

(6) Attachment(附件)(if possible)。

I enclose ××× for your reference. 我附加了×××供您阅读。

Attached please find ×××. ×××在附件里。

(7) Complimentary Close(结尾敬语)。

e.g. Respectfully yours, Truly yours, Sincerely yours, Cordially yours,

## Task 1  Situation: Wang Jun sent a pair of sports shoes on www.aliexpress.com. Now he is writing an E-mail to his customer Anna Brown to write the feedback of transaction for him.

From: wangjun11007@hotmail.com
To: anna11008@hotmail.com
Subject: Feedback of the transaction
Dear Miss Anna Brown,

Thank you very much for purchasing the sports shoes on www.aliexpress.com. I have sent you the shoes and you'll receive it in one week. I hope you may give a feedback on the website after receiving the shoes. If you are satisfied with the shoes, please recommend them to other customers. Recently we've launched some news styles and you are welcome to choose and buy. When you buy for a second time, you may enjoy a special discount.

Sincerely yours,
Wang Jun

Answer the following questions about the above sample.

1. Who is the recipient of the E-mail?
   _____.
2. What is the subject of the sample E-mail?
   _____.
3. Why does the writer write this E-mail?
   _____.

**Task 2** Suppose you are Wang Ming, the sales manager, you are required to complete the E-mail based on the information given below.

1. 发件人：王明
2. 收件人：Mr. John Brown
3. 发件人电子邮件地址：wangming123@hotmail.com
4. 收件人电子邮件地址：john456@hotmail.com
5. 主题：讨论继续合作问题

内容：1. 感谢对方订购了你公司的新款沙发床；
   2. 所订购的货物已发出，大约3天后到达；
   3. 收到货物后请回复；
   4. 希望能继续与对方合作。

E-mail Message

To: 1 _____
From: 2 _____
Subject: 3 _____

Dear 4 _____,

5 _____.
6 _____.
Please give us a reply after receiving the goods.
The efforts you have made impress me a lot. Thanks again for your contact with us and we are looking forward to 7 _____ very soon.

8 _____
9 _____

# Unit 6  Transportation

> **Goals**
> 
> In this unit, we will learn to:
> 1. talk about transportation, traffic, travel among cities;
> 2. have a good command of English expressions on transportation;
> 3. get familiar with the transportation trend in the future;
> 4. write a telephone message.

## Part Ⅰ  Listening & Speaking

**Task 1**  Look and say: Look at the following pictures and choose the right letters (A—F) to match the pictures below.

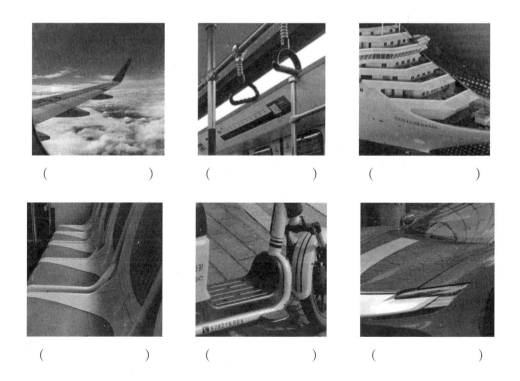

(　　　)　　(　　　)　　(　　　)

(　　　)　　(　　　)　　(　　　)

| A. subway | B. bus | C. car |
|---|---|---|
| D. scooter | E. plane | F. ship |

**Task 2** Listen and answer: You will hear two conversations. After each conversation, you will hear some questions. Choose the best answer to each question.

**Conversation 1**

1. A. It wouldn't start.          B. It ran out of gas.
   C. It was broken.              D. It was missing.
2. A. It is out of battery.       B. It is still new.
   C. It is of good quality.      D. It was bought a year.
3. A. To recharge it.             B. To repair it.
   C. To return it.               D. To sell it.

**Conversation 2**

4. A. She ran the red light.      B. She drove too fast.
   C. She had a traffic accident. D. She drove drunk.
5. A. She was sick.               B. She drank some beer.
   C. She didn't see the traffic light. D. She was in a hurry.
6. A. Her credit card.            B. Her driving license.
   C. Her insurance policy.       D. Her passport.

**Task 3** Listen and fill: Listen to the dialogue below twice and fill in the blanks. Then discuss with your partner: Should you choose public transport or private vehicles to go to work?

Sam: Hi, Jill! I heard that you moved from downtown to the suburban areas to live.

Jill: Yes, I did. I moved two months ago. The air is fresher, and the rent is 1 _____ _____.

Sam: As far as I know, your company is located in the downtown area. How do you manage to get to 2 _____ _____ _____ every day?

Jill: I bought a car. And the facilities around my house are getting changed and make it 3 _____ _____ to commute (通勤).

Sam: Sounds good. What is it like?

Jill: When I need gas for my car, I pull into a gas station right 4 _____ _____ _____ from my house and use my gas card. Years ago, full-service gas stations were very 5 _____.

Sam: Yes, now most gas stations are self-service 6 _____ and you can avoid a long line.

Jill: Personally, I 7 _____ fill the car up with gas every time I stop. I generally 8 _____ _____ _____, but more and more gas stations accept credit cards.

Sam: Have you considered the gas price as well? You know gas prices are 9_____ _____ _____.

Jill: True. The good news is that a new subway line is opening near my community（社区）very soon. So I'm now thinking about buying a more fuel-efficient（省油）vehicle or just 10 _____ _____ _____ to work.

Sam: I bet you do.

## Task 4　Discuss and debate.

People hold different opinions about public transportation. Do you think it is a good or bad choice for commuters?

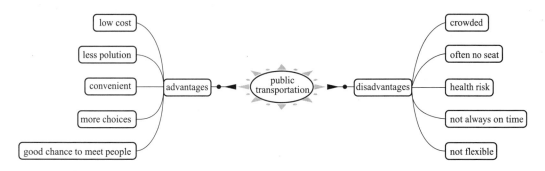

# Part Ⅱ　Text 1

## Preview Questions

**Work in pairs and discuss the following questions.**

1. What transport vehicles have you taken to different places?
2. Why do you choose them?
3. What transport vehicles may come into existence in the future?

## Background Information

With the development and expansion（扩张）of cities, commuting across the city is commonplace. However, as more commuters are employed in big cities, will the transport system break down? The following article will give you some hints.

### What your commute will look like in 2050[①]

By 2050 the world will be urban. Nearly 70% of the world's population will live in cities.

---

① 本文改编自网站爱语吧 2/15/2020 BBC 新闻，原文网址 http://m.iyuba.cn/news.html？id=31856&type=bbc. 又见 Note 1 说明。

Many of them are big cities with populations of more than 10 million.

Moving people around from place to place will be a huge challenge. The average traffic speed in central London has fallen to about 7 miles per hour. Around the same speed it was 150 years ago, in the days of the horse and cart.

But city planners are working on solutions to the traffic problem. Self-driving cars will play a part. It's predicted there will be more than 30 million self-driving cars on the road by 2040. Self-driving vehicles are already in operation in controlled areas, for example, as airport shuttles.

By 2050, city streets are likely to be filled with robo-taxis that we can get at a single touch. Public transport will be highly personalized. No more searching and following the bus timetable, instead Internet-connected transport shuttles will just route themselves according to where the passengers need to go. That slow last mile of travel may shift to two wheels. Electric scooters and bikes schemes will be popular. They're still illegal in many places with safety concerns, but cities could build special lanes to accommodate riders. Xiamen in southeast China already has an 8-kilometer above-road cycle way, and cities worldwide are designing much longer covered tubes to protect riders high above city streets. That's another likely feature of urban transport in 2050. It will be multi-level.

Companies like Uber and Lilium Jet are planning flying taxis and electric jets that can take off vertically from <u>landing pads</u> around the city. Underground systems may include the hyperloop with travel pods moving rapidly down vacuum-sealed tubes at high speed. All that might mean more space at ground level. Many cities are already turning some central streets into walking-on-foot zones.

Urban transport in 2050 might, for many people, return to the oldest form of all.

## New Words

*commute/kəˈmjuːt/  v. 通勤；因工作而往返于两地

urban/ˈɜː(r)bən/  adj. 城市的；都市的

population/ˌpɒpjuˈleɪʃn, ˌpɑːpjuˈleɪʃn/  n. 人口；人口数量

average/ˈævərɪdʒ/ adj. 平均的；一般的；通常的
predict/prɪˈdɪkt/ v. 预言；预报；预测
*shuttle/ˈʃʌtl/ n. 穿梭车
personalize/ˈpɜː(r)sənəlaɪz/ v. 个性化
illegal/ɪˈliːgl/ adj. 非法的；不合法的
lane/leɪn/ n. 小道；小巷
accommodate/əˈkɒmədeɪt, əˈkɑːmədeɪt/ v. 使适应；容纳
tube/tuːb/ n. 管道
electric/ɪˈlektrɪk/ n. 电动的；带电的
*vertically/ˈvɜː(r)tɪkli/ adv. 垂直地
pad/pæd/ n. （起飞）台
*hyperloop/ˈhaɪpəluːp/ n. 超回路；超回线
vacuum/ˈvækjuːm/ n. 真空
sealed/siːld/ adj 密封的

**Phrases and Expressions**

from place to place 从一处到另一处
fall to 跌至
play a part 起作用
self-driving cars 无人驾驶汽车
be in operation 在运转中；在实施中
be likely to 可能的；要发生的
multi-level 多层面的
turn...into... 把……转变为……

**Proper Nouns**

Uber/ˈuːbər/ 优步（美国硅谷的一家科技公司，以其打车优步 App 而出名）
Lilium/ˈliliəm/ 德国一家飞行出租公司


**Notes**

1. What your commute will look like 是来自 BBC 公司的一则语音新闻，旨在探讨未来通勤之路上的改革和创新。本文为语音抄本，对其中的字句做了微调以适应使用者的英语水平。

2. Around the same speed it was 150 years ago, in the days of the horse and cart. 本句是把伦敦闹市高峰区的通勤速度与 150 年前的马车行驶速度进行对比，用到的是原级比较，"the same...as it was" 省略了 as，十分诙谐地揭示了伦敦当前交通高峰拥堵时期的通勤速度之慢。

3. By 2050, city streets are likely to be filled with robo-taxis that we can get at a single

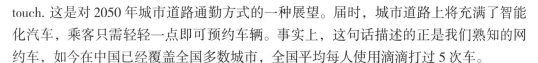

touch. 这是对 2050 年城市道路通勤方式的一种展望。届时，城市道路上将充满了智能化汽车，乘客只需轻轻一点即可预约车辆。事实上，这句话描述的正是我们熟知的网约车，如今在中国已经覆盖全国多数城市，全国平均每人使用滴滴打过 5 次车。

4. They're still illegal in many places with safety concerns, but cities could build special lanes to accommodate riders. 本句前半句采用的是一般现在时，对现状进行描述，出于安全的考虑，目前在许多地方，这两种车还不能合法上路。后半句 could 一词的使用，语气转换成虚拟，暗示城市可以为这部分骑行者规划专门的道路。

5. Underground systems may include the hyperloop with travel pods moving rapidly down vacuum-sealed tubes at high speed. 本句的描述也是一种展望，may 一词体现可能、可以。当下的技术已经让地下通道即地铁成为可能，而在这个基础上设计成真空中运行的超级高铁，提升速度，也不是不可能的。

## Task 1　Answer the following questions according to the text.

1. What will the world be like by 2050?

2. What will the traffic be like in central London in 2050?

3. How many cars predicted will be on the road by 2040?

4. What special roads have been built in Xiamen?

5. What will Uber and Lilium plan to produce?

## Task 2　Choose the best answer for each of the following questions or statements according to the text.

1. According to the text, what makes future urban commuting a huge challenge?
    A. The influx of population to cities.
    B. The traffic speed is falling to 7 miles per hour.
    C. The invention of more than 30 million cars.
    D. The construction of special roads.
2. Which of the following is NOT a solution to traffic problems in the future?
    A. Self-driving cars
    B. Robo-taxis
    C. Personalized public transport
    D. Motorcycles

3. What is true according to the text?
   A. Cities worldwide have built much longer covered tubes to protect riders high above city streets.
   B. Uber is the only company that is planning to produce modern vehicles such as flying taxis and electric jets.
   C. Multi-level transport roads will be built to accommodate different riders in the future.
   D. Travel pods will replace the current underground system.
4. What is the best replacement to the underlined phrase "landing pads" in the last but one paragraph?
   A. a large floating leaf
   B. platform for landing
   C. paper sheet
   D. cushion
5. What does the last paragraph imply?
   A. Many people might return to the countryside to live in 2050.
   B. Most people may give up commuting in 2050.
   C. Many people may walk instead of taking any vehicles to work.
   D. Most people might take the flying taxis or electric jets to work.

## Task 3  反身代词（Reflexive Pronouns）：

| 人称 | 单数 | 复数 |
| --- | --- | --- |
| 第一人称 | myself 我自己 | ourselves 我们自己 |
| 第二人称 | yourself 你自己 | yourselves 你们自己 |
| 第三人称 | himself 他自己<br>herself 她自己<br>itself 它自己 | themselves 他/她/它们自己 |

**Fill in the blanks with the reflective pronouns given below, and each one can be used only once.**

A. myself   B. yourself   C. himself   D. herself   E. itself   F. ourselves   G. yourselves
H. themselves

1. In 1955 Walt Disney _____ opened the first Disney park.
2. Maria bought _____ a scarf.
3. We must look after _____ very well.
4. Please help _____ to some fish.
5. The thing _____ is not important.
6. I _____ drove the car.
7. They dressed _____ up quickly and left the house.
8. Take care not to hurt yourselves.

# Part III  Grammar Focus

## 主谓一致（Subject-verb Agreement）

在句子中谓语动词的数必须和主语的数保持主谓一致。

判断的三个原则：

1. 语法一致原则。

主语是单数，谓语动词用单数；主语是复数，谓语动词用复数。

例如：Xiamen in southeast China already has an 8-kilometer above-road cycle way, and cities worldwide are designing much longer covered tubes.

（前半句的主语是厦门，视为单数，谓语动词用has；后半句主语是cities，为复数，谓语则用到are。）

2. 意义一致原则。

主语形式为单数，意义是复数，谓语动词用复数；主语形式为复数，意义是单数，谓语动词用单数。

例如：Nearly 70% of the world's population are living in cities.

（population 形式上是单数，但意思上指的是人口的数量，因此谓语动词要用复数are。）

同样用法的还有 people，cattle 等集体名词。形式复数意义单数的词多见于学科或领域词汇，例如 maths，politics，physics，谓语应采用单数。

3. 就近一致原则。

谓语动词的单复数形式取决于最靠近它的主语。比较：

There is an electric scooter and two robo-taxis in the parking lot.

There are two electric scooters and a robo-taxi in the parking lot.

在这两句话中，离 there be 最近的主语决定了 be 动词是用 is 还是 are。

## Task 1  Put the right forms in the brackets.

1. If anyone _____ (see) Lisa, ask her to call.
2. Each of the students _____ (have) an apple.
3. The students each _____ (have) an apple.
4. All _____ (be) equal before the law.
5. All _____ (be) well that ends well.
6. Having to change trains _____ (be) a small inconvenience.
7. More than one student _____ (have) failed the exam.
8. The rich _____ (be) to help the poor.

9. Not only the students but also the teacher _____ ( wish ) for a holiday.

10. There _____ ( be ) a cup of tea and some apples on the table.

## Task 2   Choose the correct answer and underline the noun clauses.

1. If anyone _____ Lisa, ask her to call.
    A. see            B. will see         C. sees          D. saw

2. Reading aloud _____ very important in learning English.
    A. are            B. being            C. am            D. is

3. Many a page _____ missing in the book.
    A. being          B. are              C. will be       D. is

4. The Chinese _____ hard-working.
    A. is             B. are              C. will have     D. is going to be

5. Physics _____ my favorite subject.
    A. must be        B. be               C. are           D. is

6. Three sheep _____ eating grass there.
    A. is             B. are              C. has           D. have

7. The class _____ doing experiments.
    A. be             B. is               C. are           D. have

8. Not his parents but he _____ want to go.
    A. don't          B. are              C. is            D. doesn't

9. _____ either you or he fit for the job?
    A. Are            B. Is               C. Do            D. Does

10. Tom as well as two of his friends _____ invited to the party.
    A. were           B. was              C. do            D. does

## Task 3   Link words together into a sentence.

1. of/I/is/the/difficulty/one/am/not/afraid/who/.

_____

2. Picasso/on/pictures/the/by/wall/some/hang/.

_____

3. is/responsible/the/boys/it/are/accident/for/who/the/.

_____

4. when/finish/could/task/the/is/known/they/not/yet/.

_____

## Part Ⅳ  Text 2

### Preview Questions

**Work in pairs and discuss the following questions.**

1. What transport vehicles do you take to go home from school?
2. Is it easy or difficult for you to get a transport ticket during the Spring Festival?
3. How do you usually get the ticket during the Spring Festival Travel Rush?

**Background Information**

The Spring Festival is one of the most important Chinese traditional festivals. Many people have saved up a whole year to spend the time and money with their family members. As a large population of people are working in the city to make a living and need to return home by public transport, what can the country do to maintain a safe and fast transport system during the Spring Festival Travel Rush? Get some hints from the article below.

## Spring Festival Travel Rush:
## Growth of Transportation Network[①]

China will better cope this year with the heavy traffic during the Spring Festival travel rush, with some 3 billion trips set to be made, as technologies from cloud computing to artificial intelligence kicked in to help cope with the traffic jam.

The 40-day travel rush that started on Friday unleashed the world's largest annual human migration—15 days ahead of the Lunar New Year—as families reunite for China's most important traditional holiday.

In a bid to better manage the traffic peak, the Ministry of Transport said it will make full use of technologies such as big data to enhance connectivity and efficiency between multiple modes of transportation by sending more public transport vehicles, buses and taxis to transportation centers including railway stations, airports and tourist attractions.

---

① 本文改编自网站爱语吧 1/11/2020 英语头条新闻,原文网址 http://m.iyuba.cn/news.html? id=11342&type=news.

Alibaba Cloud, the nation's top cloud computing provider, has also introduced a suite of service including data analytics, stronger computing power and the Internet of things to help take the stress out of the festive journeys.

"Machine learning manages to identify any accidents or malfunctions in real time, which is much more efficient than the human eye," said Zhao Shengqiang, a senior engineer responsible for Alibaba Cloud architecture.

Didi Chuxing, an online car-renting company, also said it will keep applying artificial intelligence technologies to detect driver fatigue during the travel rush as part of efforts to reduce accidents and ease traffic congestion.

**New Words**

traditional/trəˈdɪʃənl/ adj. 传统的
*unleashed/ʌnˈliːʃt/ v. 解除……的束缚；释放
*migration/maɪˈɡreɪʃn/ n. 移民；移往；移动
reunite/ˌriːjuːˈnaɪt/ v. 再结合；再统一；重聚
bid/bɪd/ n. 出价；努力
*enhance/ɪnˈhæns/ v. 加强
connectivity/kəˌnekˈtɪvəti/ n. 连通性
efficiency/ɪˈfɪʃnsi/ n. 效率；功率
*multiple/ˈmʌltɪpl/ adj. 多种多样的
identify/aɪˈdentɪfaɪ/ v. 识别；辨认出
malfunction/ˌmælˈfʌŋkʃn/ n. 故障；失灵
apply/əˈplaɪ/ v. 应用
detect/dɪˈtekt/ v. 发觉；察觉
*fatigue/fəˈtiːɡ/ n. 疲劳；疲乏
ease/iːz/ v. 减轻

**Phrases and Expressions**

cope with 应对
cloud computing 云计算
artificial intelligence 人工智能
kick in 开始生效
traffic peak 交通高峰期
make full use of 充分利用
tourist attractions 旅游胜地
data analytics 数据分析
Internet of things 物联网

**Proper Nouns**

    Spring Festival Travel Rush　春运

    Lunar New Year　春节

    Ministry of Transport　交通部

    Alibaba Cloud　阿里云

    Didi Chuxing　滴滴出行

**Notes**

    1. Spring Festival Travel Rush: Growth of transportation network. 本文来自英语头条的一则新闻报道。随着网络和大数据的发展，中国的春运成为万众瞩目的一个大事件。本报道比较客观真实地介绍了中国为应对春运所采取的措施，也给世界互联网界对大数据的运用树立了一个良好的榜样。

    2. The 40-day travel rush that started on Friday unleashed the world's largest annual human migration. 本句提出了整篇报道最重要的话题：春运。"为期40天的春运，堪称世界上最大的人类年度迁徙活动，本周五正式拉开序幕。"如何高效维持交通的运力，维护社会的稳定和秩序，是对中国的考验，也是对世界的考验。

    3. Machine learning manages to identify any accidents or malfunctions in real time, which is much more efficient than the human eye. 这句话的意思是，机器学习能够实时识别任何事故或故障，其效率远远高于人眼。这个做法正是大数据运用的精髓，用机器监控取代人工监控，提高监控的准确性和效率。

## Multiple-Choice Questions

**Choose the best answer for each of the following questions or statements according to the text.**

1. What Chinese festival is involved in this travel rush?

    A. the Spring Festival                   B. the Mid-Autumn Day

    C. the Lantern Festival                 D. the Dragon Boat Festival

2. How many days does the travel rush last?

    A. 3 days                                   B. 40 days

    C. 15 days                                 D. not mentioned

3. What method will the Ministry of Transport use to manage the traffic peak?

    A. All transport vehicles

    B. Public transport vehicles

    C. Technologies such as big data

    D. Data analytics, stronger computing power and the Internet of things.

4. How can artificial intelligence technologies help manage traffic?

A. By identifying any accidents or malfunctions in real time.

B. By enhancing connectivity and efficiency between multiple modes of transportation.

C. By detecting driver fatigue.

D. All above.

# Part V  Exercises

## Task 1  Vocabulary and Structure.

**Section A   Multiple Choice.**

**Directions:** Complete each one by deciding on the most appropriate word or words from the four choices.

1. By 2050 the world _____ urban.
   A. is          B. will be          C. is going to be          D. shall be
2. Near half of the world's _____ will be affected by water shortage.
   A. population                      B. transportation
   C. communication                   D. conversation
3. Moving so many people around from place to place will be a huge _____.
   A. change      B. chance           C. challenge       D. cheers
4. Self-driving cars will _____ to solve the traffic problem.
   A. play a game B. take part        C. make a part     D. play a part
5. City streets are likely to be filled ____ robo-taxis that we can get at a single touch.
   A. for         B. on               C. with            D. in
6. Motorcycles are still _____ in many places with safety concerns.
   A. illegal     B. important        C. possible        D. available
7. China will _____ with the heavy traffic this year better.
   A. come along  B. care             C. cope            D. put up
8. The government will make full use _____ technologies such as big data to enhance connectivity among cities.
   A. to          B. of               C. on              D. with
9. Machine learning is more _____ than human eyes to identify accidents or malfunctions in real time.
   A. efficient                       B. effort
   C. inefficient                     D. efficiency
10. The car-renting company will keep _____ artificial intelligence technologies to detect driver fatigue.

## Unit 6  Transportation

A. apply　　　　B. application　　　　C. applicable　　　　D. applying

**Section B　Blank Filling.**

　　**Directions**: There are five incomplete statements here. You should fill in the blanks with the proper forms of the words given in the brackets.

11. Spring Festival travel rush is a result of the festive family ＿＿＿＿＿＿（reunite）.
12. Alibaba Cloud has ＿＿＿＿＿＿（introduce）a suite of service to help ease traffic.
13. China is ＿＿＿＿＿＿（like）to make use of the big data to control traffic in future.
14. The number of car owners is ＿＿＿＿＿＿（expect）to fall in the coming year.
15. It is ＿＿＿＿＿＿（legal）to change the car license number as you like.

## Task 2　Translation–English into Chinese.

　　**Directions**: This part, numbered 1 through 5, is to test your ability to translate English into Chinese. Each of the four sentences (No. 1 to No. 4) is followed by four choices of suggested translation marked A, B, C and D. Mark the best choice and circle the corresponding letter. Write your translation of the paragraph (No. 5) in the corresponding space.

1. Public transport will be highly personalized.
   A. 公交系统将会很大程度上被私有化。
   B. 公共交通很大程度上将会被个性化。
   C. 公交系统很有可能会有个性化的发展。
   D. 公共交通个性化的程度会很高。

2. That slow last mile of travel may shift to two wheels.
   A. 那缓慢的最后一英里的旅途可能会被两个轮子所代替。
   B. 双轮车可能会取代那缓慢的最后一英里的旅途。
   C. 最后一英里的缓慢出行也许会换成双轮车。
   D. 两个轮子可能是解决最后一英里的缓慢旅途的办法。

3. Technologies from cloud computing to artificial intelligence will kick in to help cope with the traffic jam.
   A. 来自云计算和人工智能的技术将生效来帮忙应对交通堵塞。
   B. 来自云计算和人工智能的技术已被广泛使用在交通堵塞问题的治理上。
   C. 云计算和人工智能技术会用于应对交通堵塞的问题。
   D. 云计算和人工智能技术将开始生效以应对堵塞的交通。

4. Many cities are already turning some central streets into walking–on–foot zones.
   A. 不少城市已经在改造中心区域的步行区。
   B. 在许多城市里，一些中心街区已经变成步行区。
   C. 许多城市已经将部分中心街区改造成了步行区。

D. 很多城市已经把一些中心街区变成行人区域。

5. The 40-day travel rush that started on Friday unleashed the world's largest annual human migration–15 days ahead of the Lunar New Year–as families reunite for China's most important traditional holiday.

## Part Ⅵ  Writing: Telephone Message（电话留言）

电话留言是便条的一种，是一种方便接电话者快速记下电话内容并清晰传递给不在场的信息接收者的非正式文体。有些公司的电话留言条还有专用的表格方便接电话者填写。下方是一个常见的电话留言条的填写表格：

| From | | Telephone | |
| --- | --- | --- | --- |
| To | | Department | |
| Time | | | |
| Message | | | |
| Handling suggestion | | | |

**Sample 1**

Telephone Message
To: _____Thomas Watsons（Sales Manager）_____
in your absence
Mr./Ms. _____Lilian Fort_____ of _____Emerson Lighting LTD. Co._____
Telephone No. _____665-629-836-00_____
and left the following message
_____She got stuck in traffic and may be late for the 10:00AM meeting.
She will have to rearrange the meeting time with you and give you a
call later in the afternoon._____
Signed: _____Lucy_____    Date: _____Dec. 20_____ Time: _____9:30AM_____

## Sample 2

```
                    TELEPHONE NOTES
To Claire Wolf
Date Dec. 20   Time 9:30AM
                  WHILE YOU WERE OUT
Mr/Mrs/Ms Wallet
Of Morning Post
Phone No. 3888-8888
  ☐ TELEPHONED           ☑ WILL CALL AGAIN
  ☑ CALLED TO SEE YOU    ☐ PLEASE CALL HIM/HER
  ☐ WANTS TO SEE YOU     ☑ URGENT
Message
        She is a reporter from Morning Post and she's called three times. Says it can't wait.
        Something about the copier we sold that didn't work. Pls phone her ASAP.
Sign Lynn
```

## Sample 3

May, 2020

Mr. Green,

Here is a message from the Dean of English Department, who has telephoned at 8:40 this morning. He will be expecting you at 10:00 tomorrow morning in his office. Please call him back if the time doesn't suit you. His phone number is 856539.

Jacky

**Useful patterns**

1. sb. has just rung up saying that...   某人刚刚来电话说……

2. sth. about...   关于……的事情

3. Please call sb. at ( telephone number ) about sth.   请打电话给某人说关于某事，他/她的电话号码是……

4. Here is a message from sb. for you.   这是某某给你的电话留言。

5. He said he would ring later again.   他说他会再打电话过来。

6. Please ring him as soon as possible.   请尽快给他回电话。

**Task 1  Fill in the telephone message form based on the information given below.**

> The date is Dec. 5th, 2020. While Mr. Balmer was away, Mr. Bill Chunk called from Amazon. Mr. Chunk asked Mr. Balmer to call back today before 5:00 PM or any time tomorrow. The telephone number is 02-543-8812. Mr. Chunk would like to negotiate the order quantity. The message was taken by Lydia May.

```
                         Telephone Message
To: _____
From: _____  of  _____
Date: _____

Message: _____
          _____
          _____
          _____

Message taken by: _____
```

**Task 2  Fill in the telephone message based on the dialogue below. Mark the time and date on your own.**

Linda: Hello, Mr. Marble's Office. This is Linda. What can I do for you?

Mary: Hello. May I speak to Mr. Marble?

Linda: Sorry. Mr. Marble is out of town today. May I take a message?

Mary: Yes, please. I would like to make an appointment with him next week to discuss the product packing. I will be all free from Wednesday to Friday.

Linda: OK, an appointment for product packing. May I have your name, Madam?

Mary: Yes. This is Mary Johnson from ABC company. Can you ask him to call me back to confirm the time?

Linda: All right. He will call you back to confirm the time. May I have your telephone number?

Mary: Yes, it's 555-0908.

Linda: 555-0908.

Mary: That's right.

Linda: OK, Ms. Johnson. I will pass him the message as soon as he comes back. Is there anything else I can do for you?

Mary: Well, yes, it's about...

...

TELEPHONE NOTES

To _____

Date _____ Time _____

WHILE YOU WERE OUT

Mr/Mrs/Ms. _____

Of _____

Phone No. _____

☐ TELEPHONED          ☐ WILL CALL AGAIN

☐ CALLED TO SEE YOU   ☐ PLEASE CALL HIM/HER

☐ WANTS TO SEE YOU    ☐ URGENT

Message

_____

_____

Sign _____

# Unit 7　Marketing

**Goals**

In this unit, we will learn to:

1. talk about the marketing campaigns that have impressed us;
2. have a good command of English expressions on marketing;
3. get familiar with an advertisement and a leaflet;
4. write a leaflet.

## Part Ⅰ　Listening & Speaking

**Task 1**　Look and say: Look at the following pictures and choose the right letters (A—F) to match the pictures below.

(　　　)

(　　　)

(　　　)

(　　　)

(　　　)

(　　　)

# Unit 7  Marketing

A. product    B. price    C. promotion
D. place    E. advertisement    F. leaflet

**Task 2  Listen and say**: You will hear two conversations. After each conversation, you will hear some questions. Choose the best answer to each question.[①]

**Conversation 1**

1. A. Product    B. Price
   C. Promotion    D. Place
2. A. Last year    B. The year before last
   C. Last month    D. This year
3. A. Because they are not in fashion now
   B. Because they are black
   C. Because they are Size Five
   D. Because they look uncomfortable

**Conversation 2**

4. A. Product    B. Price
   C. Promotion    D. Place
5. A. Eight hundred pounds    B. Three hundred pounds
   C. Two hundred pounds    D. Fifty pounds
6. A. A month    B. Fifty months
   C. Eight months    D. Twelve months

**Task 3  Listen and fill**: Listen to the dialogue below twice and fill in the blanks. After listening, read the dialogue below carefully and act it out with your partner.[②]

An employee from the ABC Business Consultant Firm is interviewing a consumer on the street. They want to find out which of the 4 Ps influences customers' decision on purchasing.

Employee: Excuse me, miss. I'm from the ABC Business Consultant Firm. Here's my card. May I ask you a few questions?

Consumer: Why?

Employee: We are conducting a 1 _____ research. We want to find out which of the four Ps influences your 2 _____ on purchasing. This information will help us with

---

[①] 本文改编自《新概念英语1》/（英）亚历山大，何其莘著．北京：外语教学与研究出版社，2019.11，P153，225.

[②] 本文改编自《商务英语口语（第3版）》/房玉靖，梁晶主编．北京：清华大学出版社，2019.2，P67-68.

our further marketing policy and you aren't 3 _____ _____ any risks.

Consumer: The four Ps?

Employee: Yeah. It 4 _____ _____ product, the goods or services you buy; the price, the money you pay for the goods or services; 5 _____, informing you about the products and persuading you to buy them; the place, where products are available.

Consumer: Hmmm... All right.

Employee: Thank you. May I know your occupation, please.

Consumer: I am a teacher.

Employee: I see. What products have you bought recently?

Consumer: Some cosmetics.

Employee: May I know why you bought them? I mean which of the four Ps influenced your decision to buy.

Consumer: Well, let me see. Hmmm... I bought them in a discount store near 6 _____ I live. I'd seen some advertising on a social media platform for a new facial mask. There was a free sample and I tried it and liked it. Of course, it's not as pleasant as 7 _____ in a department store, but I saved at least 30% on the 8 _____ _____. Anyway, parking near the department store in the city is not very easy and the discount store is just 9 _____ _____ _____, so apart from the price, the place was important factor 10 _____ _____.

Employee: And you were attracted by the advertisement and the free sample at first, right?

Consumer: Yes. It's really nice.

Employee: I see. So promotion is important to you, too.

Consumer: Hmmm... In the way I know it, I think so.

Employee: OK. Thank you for your time. Have a nice day!

## Task 4  Discuss and share your experience with your partner according to the mind map and information below.[①]

What is a marketing campaign? Have you ever been impressed by a marketing campaign? Match the numbers (1—4) to the definitions (A—D) and then tell your partner about a marketing campaign that impressed you on the mind map as well as the information below.

---

[①] 本文改编自 wisegeek, 01/08/2021; 作者 John Lister; 原文网址 https://www.wisegeek.com/what-is-a-marketing-campaign.htm

# Unit 7  Marketing

Marketing as a whole is a continuous ongoing process of trying to create awareness of a product, service or company, specifically awareness that is in a positive manner. A marketing campaign is more restricted and usually involves a time limit and a budget, as well as a specific goal. It will often concentrate on one aspect of a business or organization's work, such as a new or revised product.

(    ) 1. a marketing campaign

(    ) 2. public relations

(    ) 3. direct marketing

(    ) 4. advertising

A. It involves communicating directly with consumers, for example through leaflets, E-mail messages, mailed letters or mobile messaging.

B. It is paying the operators of a communications service such as television, radio or newspapers to carry a message.

C. It is comprised of a number of activities carried out to accomplish a specific goal, most commonly the promotion of a product or service.

D. It is working to have media outlets mention the product, service or message in their editorial content.

# Part Ⅱ  Text 1

## Preview Questions

**Work in pairs and discuss the following questions.**

1. Have you ever been attracted to some store by scent? Why or Why not?
2. How do you understand marketing? Would you please give an example?
3. What is the purpose of marketing?

**Background Information**

Marketing is the process of teaching consumers why they should choose your product or service over those of your competitors, and is a form of persuasive communication. If the objective of your business is to sell more products or services, then marketing is what helps you achieve that goal. Anything that you use to communicate with your customers in a way that persuades them to buy your products or services is marketing. Marketing is everywhere. While traditional marketing catches your eyes and ears, there's another industry quietly fighting for your attention. And they're doing it through your nose.

## How Marketers Target Your Nose[①]

Scent marketing is the idea to combine all the touch points of the customer experience with scent. It is not like a logo or something that you see everywhere, which everybody sees the same way. Due to different experiences, upbringing and growth processes, people might find the scent to be a little bit different. It's more emotional.

In fact, you've already experienced scent marketing. Once you start to be conscious of it, you'll notice that it's everywhere. When you walk into certain banks, when you walk into certain malls, when you walk into stores, all types of businesses are using it.

And you know it can have a great impact on your mind. If it's working properly, scent marketing is helping create a positive experience for both the business and the customer. For example, the coffee scent can create a refreshing feeling, even if you haven't had any coffee.

Various research over the years also found that shoppers in scented environments may stay longer, consider the goods better and are more willing to pay higher prices. People are actually more comfortable. They feel warm. They feel invited. They feel welcomed. It's really creating an amazing experience for customers when they walk in.

But scent marketing is a bit more complicated.

In 2008, Starbucks had to put the sale of breakfast sandwiches on hold. The sandwich smell was competing with the coffee scent, ruining the atmosphere. Think about that. If a coffee shop doesn't smell like coffee, would you still start your morning there? In the same way that scent marketing can bring a positive experience, when the scent doesn't match the population, location or brand identity, the public reaction is often negative.

### New Words

marketing/ˈmɑːkɪtɪŋ/ n. 营销；促销；销售活动
competitor/kəmˈpetɪtə(r)/ n.（尤指商业方面的）竞争者，对手；参赛者
*persuasive/pəˈsweɪsɪv/ adj. 有说服力的；令人信服的
objective/əbˈdʒektɪv/ n. 目标；目的
achieve/əˈtʃiːv/ v.（凭长期努力）达到（某目标、地位、标准）；完成；成功
persuade/pəˈsweɪd/ v. 劝说；说服；使信服

---

① 本文改编自爱语吧 06/05/2020；作者 Edward Bishop；原文网址 http://m.iyuba.cn/news.html？id=12847&type=news

traditional/trəˈdɪʃənl/ adj. 传统的；习俗的；惯例的
scent/sent/ n. 香味；（人的）气味；气息
combine/kəmˈbaɪn/ v.（使）结合；组合；联合
*upbringing/ˈʌpbrɪŋɪŋ/ n. 教养；抚育；培养
emotional/ɪˈməʊʃənl/ adj. 感情的；情感的；情绪的
experience/ɪkˈspɪəriəns/ v. 经历；经受 n. 经验；经历
conscious/ˈkɒnʃəs, ˈkɑːnʃəs/ adj. 意识到的；注意到的；神志清醒的
impact/ˈɪmpækt/ n. 巨大影响；强大作用；冲击力
properly/ˈprɒpəli, ˈprɑːpəli/ adv. 正确地；适当地；得体地
positive/ˈpɒzətɪv/ adj. 积极乐观的；自信的；积极的
various/ˈveəriəs/ adj. 各种不同的；各种各样的
complicated/ˈkɒmplɪkeɪtɪd, ˈkɑːmplɪkeɪtɪd/ adj. 复杂的；难懂的
ruin/ˈruːɪn/ v. 毁坏；破坏；糟蹋
atmosphere/ˈætməsfɪə(r)/ n. 气氛；大气；大气层
*identity/aɪˈdentəti/ n. 身份；特征
negative/ˈneɡətɪv/ adj. 坏的；消极的；负面的

**Phrases and Expressions**

communicate with 与……沟通
fight for 为……而战斗（竞争）
due to 由于
growth process 成长过程
be conscious of 意识到
have a great impact on 对……有巨大影响
put... on hold 暂停；搁置

**Notes**

1. While traditional marketing catch your eyes and ears, ... 传统的市场营销针对你的眼睛和耳朵……。任何用来说服客户购买产品或服务的过程都是市场营销，传统上包括广告、社交媒体、优惠券、销售，甚至包括产品的展示方式等。

2. In 2008, Starbucks had to put the sale of breakfast sandwiches on hold. 在 2008 年，星巴克不得不暂停出售早餐三明治。2003 年，星巴克开始销售三明治，但三明治不可避免地在烤箱中吱吱作响并散发出的气味和星巴克的咖啡文化不符，所以在 2008 年被停止了销售。

## Task 1  Answer the following questions according to the text.

1. What is scent marketing?

2. Where might you have experienced scent marketing?

3. How does scent marketing create a positive experience for customers?

4. Why may shoppers in scented environments stay longer?

5. Compared to traditional marketing, why is scent marketing a bit more complicated?

## Task 2  Choose the best answer for each of the following questions or statements according to the text.

1. Scent marketing is the idea to combine all the touch points of the customer experience _____ scent.
   A. to  B. with  C. of  D. in

2. It's really creating an amazing experience for customers when they walk in. Amazing experience doesn't include_____.
   A. They feel warm             B. They feel invited
   C. They feel refreshed        D. They feel welcomed

3. People's reaction to scent _____ their experiences, upbringing and growth processes.
   A. due to                     B. depends on
   C. is conscious of            D. has a great impact on

4. When the scent doesn't match the population, location or brand identity, the public reaction is often _____.
   A. negative  B. surprised  C. amazed  D. positive

5. What is this text mainly about?
   A. The difference between traditional marketing and scent marketing.
   B. The positive impact of scent marketing.
   C. The negative impact of scent marketing.
   D. The definition of scent marketing.

## Task 3　否定前缀（Negative Prefixes）：

| 词缀 | 位置 | 意义 | 例词 |
| --- | --- | --- | --- |
| im- | 加在字母 m，b，p 之前 | 不、无、非 | impossible（不可能的），impolite（不礼貌的），impudence（厚颜无耻） |
| in- | 加在形容词、名词之前 | 不、无、非 | incorrect（不正确的），inability（无能，无力），inaccurate（不准确的） |
| ir- | 加在以 r 开头的词前 | 不、无、非 | irregular（不稳定的），irresistible（不可抵抗的），irresolvable（不能分解的，不能解决的） |
| un- | 加在名词、形容词、副词之前 | 不、无、非 | unfinished（未完成的），undoubted（无疑的），unemployment（失业） |
| non- | 加在形容词、名词前 | 不、非、无 | non-existence（不存在），non-essential（不主要的），non-electrical（非电的） |
| mis- | 加在动词、名词之前 | 误、不 | misunderstand（误解），misjudge（误判），misleading（误导），misfortune（不幸） |
| dis- | 加在动词之前 | 不、无、相反；分开、离、散；取消、除去、毁 | disappear（消失），disarm（解除武装），disconnect（失去联系） |
| de- | 加在名词，形容词之前 | 除去、取消、毁、非 | demobilize（遣散；使…复员）decolor（脱色，漂白）denationalize 非国有化 |
| anti- | 加在名词、形容词之前 | 反、防 | anti-Japanese（抗日战争），anti-social（厌恶社会的，反社会的），antidote（解毒药） |

According to the word formation above, please match the prefixes in Column A with the words in Column B.

| Column A | Column B | Column A | Column B |
| --- | --- | --- | --- |
| 1. im- | A. salt | 6. dis- | F. use |
| 2. in- | B. arm | 7. mis- | G. war |
| 3. ir- | C. polite | 8. de- | H. stop |
| 4. un- | D. correct | 9. anti- | I. official |
| 5. non- | E. rational | | |

# Part Ⅲ  Grammar Focus

## 状语从句（Adverbial Clause）

在主从复合句中充当状语的从句称为状语从句（副词性从句）。状语从句可以修饰主句中的谓语动词、形容词、副词或整个句子。按意义可以分为时间、地点、原因、目的、结果、条件、方式、比较、让步等状语从句。

### 一、状语从句的结构：引导词/词组 + 主谓结构

状语从句位于句首或句中时通常用逗号与主句隔开，位于句尾时可以不用逗号隔开。

When he got married, Alf was too embarrassed to say anything to his wife about his job.

You must put things where you take them.

You can contact me as soon as you get there.

### 二、状语从句分类一览表[①]

| 种类 | 连接词 | 例句 | 注意事项 |
| --- | --- | --- | --- |
| 时间状语从句 | 1. when, while, as, whenever<br>2. before, after, since, until/till, once（一旦……）, as soon as<br>3. by the time, every/each time, the moment/minute/immediately（一……就……）<br>4. hardly...when=no sooner...than（一……就……） | Once he has made up his mind, nothing can change it.<br>While we are young, we should work hard.<br>I want to talk with you as soon as I finish my work.<br>He didn't go to bed last night until he finished his work.<br>As she grew older, she began to go deaf. | 遵循"主将从现"的原则，即主句表示将来时态的意义时，从句用一般现在时。When 强调"特定时间"，while 强调时间段，有时表示对比的含义，as 多用于口语中，强调"同时" |

---

[①] 《状语从句分类一览表》摘自《英语语法革命》/ 李义启主编. 广州：南方日报出版社, 2019.7, P164–165

续表

| 种类 | 连接词 | 例句 | 注意事项 |
|---|---|---|---|
| 地点状语从句 | where（在……的地点）<br>wherever（无论何地） | Please stay where you are.<br>I may go wherever I like. | — |
| 原因状语从句 | because（因为……）<br>as/for（由于……，因为……）<br>since/now that（既然……）<br>seeing that/as（既然……）<br>considering（that）（考虑到……） | Since no one else is against it, we'll pass the law.<br>As she is now well today, I'll go myself.<br>Seeing as we are going the same way, I'll give you a lift. | because 引导的从句一般放在主句之后，且主句不可再用连词 so; because 语气最强, since 较弱, as 又次之, for 最弱 |
| 比较状语从句 | than（比……）<br>as...as...（与……一样）<br>not as/so...as...（与……不一样） | It is warmer in spring than（it is）in winter.<br>I get up as early as my parents do every morning.<br>He isn't so tall as Bill.<br>Liu Xiang runs much faster than I do. | as 和 than 引导的从句，常省去与主句中相同的部分，只留下相比较的部分；常用替代动词 do 等形式代替与主句相同的谓语部分 |
| 目的状语从句 | so that（以便……）=in order that<br>for fear that（如果……，以防……）<br>in case（以免……） | I got up early so that I could catch the first bus to school.<br>Better take more clothes in case the weather is cold. | 表示目的的 so that= in order that, 后常接 may, should, could 或 would 等 |
| 结果状语从句 | so...that（如此……以至于）<br>such...that（如此……以至于） | I was so excited that I couldn't go to sleep.<br>She spoke in such a low voice that we couldn't hear her at all. | 注意 so 和 such 后的搭配：<br>so+adj./adv. ...<br>such+(a/an)+(adj.)+n... |
| 条件状语从句 | if（如果……）<br>unless（除非……）<br>as/so long as（只要……就……）<br>on condition that（在……条件下）<br>suppose that（假如……）<br>in case（万一……） | He'll talk with me if he has time tomorrow.<br>You will fail in the exam unless you work harder.<br>Stay as long as you like.<br>Send me a message in case you have any difficulty. | 从句中的动词时态不可用将来时，只能用现在或过去时态来表示将来时 |

续表

| 种类 | 连接词 | 例句 | 注意事项 |
|---|---|---|---|
| 方式状语从句 | as if =as though（好像/似乎……）<br>as（像；如；按……） | We heard a noise, as if someone were breathing.<br>It looks as though it is going to rain this evening.<br>She will do as she is told. | as if/as though 引导的从句一般用虚拟语气 |
| 让步状语从句 | although, though（尽管/虽然……）<br>even if/though（即便……）<br>no matter what/who/which/how（无论什么/谁/哪个/怎样……）<br>as(尽管……，用在倒装句中) | They kept on working, though it was raining.<br>No matter how difficult (it may be), we must go on.<br>Young/Child as he is, he knows a lot. | as 作"尽管"讲，用于让步状语从句时，需用部分倒装结构，而 although/though 则用正常语序。两者可和 yet 连用，但不可与 but 连用 |

## Task 1　Find out the following sentences in the text and underline the adverbial clauses.

Once you start to be conscious of it, you'll notice that it's everywhere. When you walk into certain banks, when you walk into certain malls, when you walk into stores, all types of businesses are using it.

If it's working properly, scent marketing is helping create a positive experience for both the business and the customer. For example, the coffee scent can create a refreshing feeling, even if you haven't had any coffee.

## Task 2　Choose the correct answer and underline the attributive clauses.

1. _____ Tom came in, I was reading an interesting book.
   A. When　　　　B. While　　　　C. Till　　　　D. Until
2. _____ we got there, it began to snow.
   A. If　　　　B. While　　　　C. Time　　　　D. As soon as
3. _____ you know it, you will love it.
   A. Once　　　　B. Before　　　　C. While　　　　D. As
4. _____ you invite me, I'll go with you.
   A. For　　　　B. Since　　　　C. But　　　　D. Why
5. Successful _____ he is, he is not proud.
   A. if　　　　B. as　　　　C. when　　　　D. whatever

6. He gave us _____ good advice that we finished the task easily.
   A. so              B. such            C. that             D. if
7. _____ may happen, I won't change my mind.
   A. Although        B. Though          C. What             D. Whatever
8. Do in Rome _____ the Romans do.
   A. as              B. whatever        C. whichever        D. although
9. Speak aloud _____ I may hear you.
   A. as if           B. as though       C. so that          D. so as to
10. I always keep an umbrella in my handbag _____ it rains.
    A. if             B. in case         C. unless           D. in the event

**Task 3  Make words together into a sentence and underline the adverbial clauses.**

1. more/thought/she/less/it/about/the/she/the/felt/.

_____

2. the/book/didn't/he/as/put/had/it/been/failed/I/find/to/it/where/.

_____

3. Tom/shy/quiet/is/while/and/Jack/outgoing/confident/and/very/.

_____

4. no sooner/I/gone/had/than/rang/the/outside/phone/.

_____

# Part Ⅳ  Text 2

## Preview Questions

**Work in pairs and discuss the following questions.**

1. Do you think advertising is equal to marketing? Why?
2. In order to sell a product or service, how many stages does a company go through?
3. Have you ever heard of the four Ps model of marketing? And What is it?

**Background Information**

   Marketing includes creating the product or service concept, identifying who is likely to purchase it, promoting it, and moving it through the appropriate selling channels. Companies must go through multiple stages of marketing to ensure their products or services are ready for selling, including ideation, research and testing, advertising and selling.

## The Four Ps Model of Marketing [①]

The four stages of marketing can also be mapped onto another popular marketing model known as the Four Ps of marketing. The four Ps in this model are product, price, promotion, and place.

- Product: The procedures you have in place to ensure that your products are ready for selling. Your product (or service) should fill a gap in the market, meet the needs of customers, and stand out from the competition.

- Price: The cost of purchase, including both the sticker price as well as less quantifiable trade-offs that a customer must be willing to make when they purchase your products.

- Promotion: The information you give consumers through targeted advertising to generate interest in your products. Promotions usually have one of two purposes: generate leads or initiate actual purchases.

- Place: Refers to how and where products are sold. All distribution decisions are part of your overall marketing process.

## Types of Advertising

There are many kinds of advertising that you can use to promote your business, teach customers about your products, and generate sales. Print, radio, and television campaigns are types of advertising, as are direct mail, E-mail, and Internet marketing. If you have a website, it should be optimized for search to help customers find it through search engines like Google, Yahoo!, and Bing. Newsletters, press releases, and articles are also forms of marketing used to capture leads and generate sales. Some companies also use referral marketing, where satisfied customers refer others (often for a reward) to increase business.

The rise of social media platforms has increased the importance of social media marketing, including connecting with customers on social media by persuading them to follow your business, partnering with social media influencers through product placement or paid sponsorships, and paying for advertising on platforms like Facebook or Instagram. The types of advertising that you choose will depend on your budget, type of business, and the preferences of your ideal customers.

### New Words

model/ˈmɒdl, ˈmɑːdl/ n. 模型；样式

---

[①] 本文改编自 the balance small business 01/04/2021；作者 Laura Lake；原文网址：https://www.thebalancesmb.com/what-is-marketing-2296057

Unit 7　Marketing　　133

\*promotion/prəˈməʊʃn/　n. 提升，晋升；促销，推销
procedure/prəˈsiːdʒə(r)/　n. 程序；手续；步骤
purchase/ˈpɜːtʃəs/　n.v. 购买；采购
\*quantifiable/ˈkwɒntɪfaɪəbl/　adj. 可以定量的；能量化的
\*targeted/ˈtɑːɡɪtɪd/　adj. 有针对性的；以……为目标的；定向的
\*generate/ˈdʒenəreɪt/　v. 产生；引起
\*initiate/ɪˈnɪʃieɪt/　v. 开始；发起；创始
\*distribution/ˌdɪstrɪˈbjuːʃn/　n. 分配；（商品）经销；分销
overall/ˌəʊvərˈɔːl/　adj. 全面的；综合的；总体的
campaign/kæmˈpeɪn/　n. 运动；活动；战役
\*optimize/ˈɒptɪmaɪz, ˈɑːptɪmaɪz/　v. 使最优化；充分利用
search/sɜːtʃ/　n. 搜索；搜寻；查找；检索
\*newsletter/ˈnjuːzletə(r), ˈnjuːzletə(r)/　n. 时事通信；电子报；简报；简讯
\*influencer/ˈɪnfluənsə(r)/　n. 影响者；人物；有影响力的人
budget/ˈbʌdʒɪt/　n. 预算
preference/ˈprefrəns/　n. 偏爱；爱好；喜爱

**Phrases and Expressions**
　　fill a gap　填补空白
　　stand out from the competition　在竞争中脱颖而出
　　sticker price　标价
　　make trade-offs　进行权衡
　　generate leads　产生潜在客户
　　initiate actual purchases　启动实际购买
　　distribution decisions　分销决策
　　press releases　新闻稿
　　capture leads　捕获潜在客户
　　referral marketing　推荐营销；保举营销
　　social media platforms　社交媒体平台
　　social media influencers　社交媒体影响者，网红
　　product placement　植入式广告
　　paid sponsorships　付费赞助

**Proper Names**
　　Google　谷歌（搜索引擎）
　　Yahoo!　雅虎（搜索引擎）
　　Bing　必应（微软搜索引擎）
　　Facebook　脸书

Instagram　图片分享社交应用（照片墙）

**Notes**

1. Print, radio, and television campaigns are types of advertising, as are direct mail, E-mail, and Internet marketing. 在纸上印刷、广播和电视广告都是不同类型的广告，直接邮寄的广告、电子邮件和网络营销也是。

2. The rise of social media platforms has increased the importance of social media marketing, including connecting with customers on social media by persuading them to follow your business, partnering with social media influencers through product placement or paid sponsorships, and paying for advertising on platforms like Facebook or Instagram. 社交媒体平台的兴起增加了社交媒体营销的重要性，包括通过劝说客户关注你的业务来与社交媒体上的客户建立联系，通过植入式广告或付费赞助与社交媒体影响者建立合作关系，以及在 Facebook 或 Instagram 等平台上支付广告费用。

## Multiple-Choice Questions

**Choose the best answer for each of the following questions or statements according to the text.**

1. What are the four Ps according to the text?
    A. Product, price, purchase, place
    B. Product, price, purchase, promotion
    C. Product, price, promotion, place
    D. Product, promotion, purchase, place

2. In order to make sure that your products or services are ready for selling, what characters should the products or services have?
    A. Filling a gap in the market
    B. Meeting the needs of customers
    C. Standing out from the competition
    D. All above

3. Which of the following is NOT true according to the text?
    A. The four stages of marketing, ideation, research and testing, advertising and selling is equal to another model, the four Ps
    B. Price in the four Ps model only refers to the sticker price
    C. Targeted advertising is to arise some people's interest in products or services
    D. When it comes to Place, how and where products or services are sold should be taken into careful consideration

4. Which of the following is NOT included in types of advertising mentioned in the text?

A. Internet marketing  B. radio
C. TV campaigns  D. coupons
5. What will the types of advertising that you will choose depend on?
    A. The social media influencer
    B. The social media platforms
    C. The budget, type of business and the preferences of your ideal customers
    D. The preferences of advertisers

## Part V  Exercises

### Task 1  Vocabulary and Structure.

**Section A  Multiple Choice.**

Directions: Complete each one by deciding on the most appropriate word or words from the four choices.

1. I used to travel by air a great deal when I was a boy. So I have a lot of _____ in traveling by plane.
    A. experience  B. experiences  C. experiment  D. experiments
2. While traditional marketing catches your eyes and ears, they are in fact trying to _____ your attention.
    A. pay  B. fight  C. take  D. attract
3. _____ you start to be conscious of it, you'll notice that it's everywhere.
    A. Since  B. As well as  C. As long as  D. One
4. You know it can have a great impact on your mind. And you know it can _____ you.
    A. affect  B. effect  C. affects  D. effects
5. Scent marketing can help _____ a positive experience for both the business and the customer.
    A. creating  B. creates  C. create  D. created
6. Children are like to compete _____ each other for their parents' attention and care.
    A. to  B. with  C. in  D. for
7. The four stages of marketing can also be mapped onto another popular marketing model. The four stages of marketing _____ known as the Four Ps of marketing.
    A. is  B. be  C. are  D. to be
8. The procedures you have in place to ensure that your products are ready for selling. The word ensure means _____.
    A. make sure  B. insure  C. assure  D. sure

9. Customers must _____ to buy these products or services through all types of advertising like print, radio and television campaigns.
   A. persuade            B. persuaded
   C. be persuaded        D. persuading
10. Many people expressed a strong preference _____ the social media platforms.
    A. in        B. at        C. to        D. for

**Section B  Blank Filling.**

**Directions: There are five incomplete statements here. You should fill in the blanks with the proper forms of the words given in the brackets.**

11. If the _____ (object) of your business is to sell more products or services, then marketing is what helps you achieve that goal.
12. For example, the coffee scent can create a _____ (refresh) feeling, even if you haven't had any coffee.
13. If it's working _____ (proper), scent marketing is helping create a positive experience for both the business and the customer.
14. _____ (promote) usually have one of two purposes: generate leads or initiate actual purchases.
15. Newsletters, press releases, and articles are also forms of marketing _____ (use) to capture leads and generate sales.

## Task 2  Translation–English into Chinese.

**Directions: This part, numbered 1 through 5, is to test your ability to translate English into Chinese. Each of the four sentences (No.1 to No.4) is followed by four choices of suggested translation marked A, B, C and D. Mark the best choice and circle the corresponding letter. Write your translation of the paragraph (No.5) in the corresponding space on the Sheet.**

1. It is not like a logo or something that you see everywhere, which everybody sees the same way.
   A. 它不像一个你能到处看到的标志或什么东西，而且每个人都看到的是相同的方式。
   B. 它不像一个你能到处看到的标志或什么东西，而且每个人用相同的方式来看。
   C. 它不像你到处能看到的标志或其他什么东西，每个人对这些的体验都是一样的。
   D. 它不像你到处能看到的标志或其他什么东西，每个人看到这些都是一样的。
2. If it's working properly, scent marketing is helping create a positive experience for both the business and the customer.
   A. 如果它工作正常，香味营销有助于为企业和客户创造积极的经验。

B. 如果运作正常，气味营销将有助于为企业和客户创造出积极的体验。

C. 如果它工作正常，气味营销将有助于为企业和客户都创造出积极的体验。

D. 如果运作正常，香味营销有助于为企业和客户创造积极的经验。

3. Various research over the years also found that shoppers in scented environments may stay longer, consider the goods better and are more willing to pay higher prices.

A. 多年来的各种研究还发现，在有香味的环境中购物的人们会逗留更久，对商品的考虑更好，更愿意支付更高的价格。

B. 多年来的各种研究还发现，购物者在有香味的环境中停留的时间更长，对商品的考虑更好，更愿意支付更高的价格。

C. 多年来的各种研究还发现，购物者在有香味的环境中停留的时间更长，觉得商品更好，更不愿意支付更高的价格。

D. 多年来的各种研究也发现，在有香味的环境中购物的人们会逗留更久，觉得商品更好，也更愿意支付更高的价格。

4. The sandwich smell was competing with the coffee scent, ruining the atmosphere.

A. 三明治的味道和咖啡的香气竞争，破坏了气氛。

B. 三明治的味道和咖啡的香气竞争，破坏了氛围。

C. 三明治的味道和咖啡的味道竞争，破坏了氛围。

D. 三明治的味道和咖啡的味道竞争，破坏了气氛。

5. Anything that you use to communicate with your customers in a way that persuades them to buy your products or services is marketing. Marketing is everywhere. While traditional marketing catches your eyes and ears, there's another industry quietly fighting for your attention. And they're doing it through your nose.

___

## Part Ⅵ  Writing: Leaflet and Advertisement（传单和广告）

传单和广告是商家推销自己产品或服务时运用最多的途径。现今广告的方式有很多，传单只是平面广告的一种。在商务英语中，关于传单和广告的写作要点通常包括以下几个方面：

- 标题：商品或服务的名称。

- 正文：介绍商品或者服务以吸引顾客。
- 地址：商家地址，以便客人光顾。
- 联系电话：商家联系方式，以便顾客联系。
- 邮箱或微信公众号：如有必要。

**Task 1** Read the following leaflet and advertisement. Discuss with your partner about the differences among them.

## LEAFLET

### Litchi Chai Roast Goose

Litchi Chai Roast Goose is a special traditional Cantonese recipe, in which we have specialized for 35 years. The goose is roasted with litchi firewood. With the light fragrance of litchi, it is crisp and not oily. Address: No.18 Hongtu Road, Dongguan, Guangdong Province
Telephone: 0769-86211666

## ADVERTISEMENT

### Wanted

Salesmen
Responsibility: to work in the supermarket, 6 days a week, from 9 AM to 6 PM.
Requirements: related working experience in supermarkets.
Payment to be negotiated.
Address: No.66 Hongfu Road, Dongguan, Guangdong Province
Telephone: 0791-86335678

**Task 2** According to the examples above, imagining you are a member of the Marketing Department of Starbucks, design a sales leaflet for the campaign to relaunch a kind of coffee. It should attract attention and communicate the reasons why people should buy it.

Leaflet:

___

___

___

___

Unit 7　Marketing　　139

# Unit 8　Consuming Habits

> **Goals**
> In this unit, we will learn to:
> 1. talk about consumers, consuming habits and consumer behaviour;
> 2. have a good command of English expressions on consuming;
> 3. get familiar with a questionnaire and a complaint letter;
> 4. write a complaint letter and a reply.

## Part I　Listening & Speaking

**Task 1**　Look and say: Look at the following pictures and choose the right letters (A—F) to match the pictures below.

(　　　)　　　(　　　)　　　(　　　)

(　　　)　　　(　　　)　　　(　　　)

Unit 8　Consuming Habits

A. apple　　　　　　　　　B. cherry　　　　　　　　C. strawberry

D. Shatang mandarin　　　　E. Bintang mandarin　　　 F. rough-peel mandarin

**Task 2**　Listen and say: You will hear two conversations. After each conversation, you will hear some questions. Choose the best answer to each question.

**Conversation 1**

1. A. A mobile phone　　　　　　　　　B. A laptop
   C. A car　　　　　　　　　　　　　　D. A bicycle
2. A. Its color is good　　　　　　　　　B. Its design is good
   C. Its color and design are bad　　　　D. Its color and design are good
3. A. There is still room for improvement in color
   B. There is still room for improvement in design
   C. There is still room for improvement in performance
   D. There is no room for improvement in performance

**Conversation 2**

4. A. Wasting a lot of money　　　　　　　B. It's more expensive
   C. It's no cheaper than the old material　D. Saving a lot of money
5. A. Yes, there is　　　　　　　　　　　B. No, there isn't
   C. Certainly　　　　　　　　　　　　　D. No problem
6. A. One more case　　　　　　　　　　B. One less case
   C. Just as usual　　　　　　　　　　　D. Twice as usual

**Task 3**　Listen and fill: Read the dialogue below carefully, act it out with your partner and discuss about rational consumption.①

　　Around the campus, we can commonly see some college students wear branded clothes, using the most advanced appliances such as Ipod, Iphone and Ipad.

Mike: In spite of where the money comes from, I absolutely 1 ＿＿＿ ＿＿＿ ＿＿＿ that college students consume luxuries. 2 ＿＿＿ ＿＿＿ ＿＿＿ I am concerned, we should advocate rational consumption among college students. Would you like to share some of your opinions about it?

Sam: Sure. As follows, I will share some 3 ＿＿＿. Above all, college students should have access to 4 ＿＿＿ ＿＿＿ ＿＿＿. This is a priority. Most college students, who

---

① 本文改编自完美作业网相关试题【4】英语作文大学生怎么合理消费；原文网址 https://www.wanmeila.com/question/6d1148e70a67415089.html

have already asked their parents to 5 _____ their fee, should take responsibility to afford their daily consumption, let alone luxurious consumption. In addition, it is 6 _____, rather than luxury, that counts. Seeing other students 7 _____ luxury, some students are jealous and would like to buy one themselves. This is what we call irrational consumption. Last but not least, keep 8 _____ _____ _____ each month. If you have fancy dinner this week, then you are supposed to cut down the cost next week. Also, you can 9 _____ _____ some bonus plan for yourself. If you spend less than, say, 1,500 yuan per month, then you can allow yourself a 300 yuan luxury consumption next week. The amount varies as to how much you earn and how much you have.

Mike: Thank you very much for your good points. In a word, it is 10 _____ to carry rational consumption among college students.

## Task 4　Discuss and debate according to the mind map and survey below.

What are your own consuming habits? How do you usually manage your money? Complete the questionnaire named Consuming Habits Survey and then discuss with your partner based on the mind map as well as the survey below.

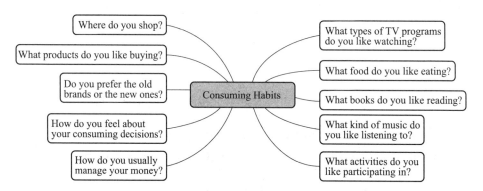

## Consuming Habits Survey[①]

Hi, Good day! Thanks for your time! It will take you 3 minutes. We are currently conducting a survey about consuming habits. We hope to get the relevant market information from you. Please help us do the survey. The questionnaire has no right or wrong answers, so please be as honest as you can. Best Wishes!

1. From your points of view, please arrange the factors in order of importance.

　　A. The design of the products　　　　　　B. The price of the products

---

① 本文改编自问卷网 – 免费模板 – 历史项目 –Consumer Habits Survey；原文网址 https://www.wenjuan.com/ssa/aMrYzq/

C. The quality of the products        D. The shopping experience

Order from the most to the least important: (   ) (   ) (   ) (   )

2. What's your age?
   A. Under 18                         B. 19
   C. 20                               D. Over 20

3. What's your gender?
   A. Female                           B. Male

4. What's your average cost on fashion items each month?
   A. Under $50                        B. $50–$99
   C. $100–$199                        D. Over $200

5. For outerwear, how much is reasonable for you?
   A. Under $50                        B. $50–$99
   C. $100–$199                        D. Over $200

6. For tops, how much is reasonable for you?
   A. Under $25                        B. $25–$99
   C. $100–$199                        D. Over $200

7. For dresses or suits, how much is reasonable for you?
   A. Under $25                        B. $25–$99
   C. $100–$199                        D. Over $200

8. For bottoms, how much is reasonable for you?
   A. Under $25                        B. $25–$99
   C. $100–$199                        D. Over $200

9. For footwear, how much is reasonable for you?
   A. Under $25                        B. $25–$99
   C. $100–$199                        D. Over $200

10. Which fashion style do you like most?
    A. Vintage fashion Style            B. Sexy fashion Style
    C. Tomboy fashion Style             D. Casual fashion Style
    E. Sophisticated fashion Style

11. If a concept shop sells brands you don't know, but the quality, style and price is to your taste, are you willing to give a try to buy it?
    A. Yes, I am                        B. No, I'm not

12. If it is a multi-brand concept store, would you prefer the collections put by colors or brands?
    A. By colors                        B. By brands

13. In fashion experience, do you have confidence in what you buy and what you wear?

A. Always do
B. Often do
C. Sometimes do
D. Seldom do
E. Never do

## Part Ⅱ　Text 1

### Preview Questions

**Work in pairs and discuss the following questions.**

1. How do you often spend your National Day holiday?

2. Where have you travelled? What do you think of them?

3. Do you often make your holiday plans? Are you quite satisfied after that? Why or why not?

### Background Information

1. China Holidays & Festivals: China has seven legal holidays in a year, including New Year's Day, Chinese New Year (the Spring Festival), the Qingming Festival, May Day, the Dragon Boat Festival, the Mid-Autumn Day and National Day. Many other galas and anniversaries are celebrated even without days off, such as Arbor Day and Teachers' Day.

2. National Day (Oct.1st): Military parade and celebration on the Tiananmen Square in Beijing; Nationwide traveling peak from Oct. 1st to 7th regarded as "the Golden Week".

3. Golden Weeks in China: Chinese New Year Holiday and National Day Holiday are the only two week-long holidays in China. During these two weeks, people enjoy themselves in a great variety of ways, contributing to a boost in tourism industry, hence the nickname "Golden Week". Hotel rooms, train tickets or air tickets will definitely be in great demand then.

4. Amidst the hustle and bustle of everyday life, it's important to be able to treat yourself to a special holiday once in a while. Whether you are a workaholic or have a busy social life, everyone should have a quick all inclusive 7 day holiday to help you relax and have some fun home or abroad. 7 days away gives you the perfect amount of time to unwind and enjoy while not keeping you away from home for too long!

## Consumer Spending up during National Holiday[①]

Chinese consumers appear to be spending more money during the National Day holiday than last year.

On the first two days of the eight-day holiday, Chinese consumers spent 628 billion yuan ($92.6 billion) by UnionPay card, up 11.8 percent year-on-year, according to UnionPay.

---

① 本文摘自 BBC NEWS 来源: iYuba 10-05-2020

On National Day, Oct 1, 2020, which overlapped with the Mid-Autumn Festival this year, transaction volume recorded by UnionPay reached 330 billion yuan, up 15.5 percent on a yearly basis, it found.

The rare extended National Day holiday has been the longest public vacation since the outbreak of the virus earlier this year. Long-distance trips and tours of western parts of China have seen growing popularity.

The Tibet autonomous region, Xinjiang Uygur autonomous region and Ningxia Hui autonomous region were the areas that saw the fastest growth of spending on a yearly basis in the first two days, the UnionPay data found.

"With vast land and lower population density, western China fits with the psychology of tourists to avoid crowds in the post-epidemic period," said Zhang Jinshan, a tourism industry professor at Beijing Union University.

On the first two days of the eight-day holiday, tourists' spending volume on hotels in Tibet more than doubled year-on-year, while spending on catering grew 49 percent. In Xinjiang, the amount spent on flight tickets tripled, and spending on admission tickets for sightseeing spots in Ningxia increased by 20 percent, according to UnionPay.

**New Words**

consumer/kənˈsuːmə(r)/ n. 消费者；用户，顾客

*overlap/ˌəʊvə(r)ˈlæp/ v. 重叠；重复

extended/ɪkˈstendɪd/ adj. 延伸的；扩大的；长期的；广大的

*outbreak/ˈaʊtbreɪk/ n. 发作；爆发，突发

virus/ˈvaɪrəs/ n. 病毒

western/ˈwestə(r)n/ adj. 西方的，西部的；有西方特征的

*popularity/ˌpɒpjuˈlærəti, ˌpɑːpjuˈlærəti/ n. 普及，流行；名气；受大众欢迎

growth/grəʊθ/ n. 增长；发展；生长；种植

population/ˌpɒpjuˈleɪʃn, ˌpɑːpjuˈleɪʃn/ n. 人口；群体；全体居民

*density/ˈdensəti/ n. 密度

*psychology/saɪˈkɒlədʒi, saɪˈkɑːlədʒi/ n. 心理学；心理状态

tourist/ˈtʊrɪst/ n. 旅行者；观光客

avoid/əˈvɔɪd/ v. 避开，躲避；消除，避免

*epidemic/ˌepɪˈdemɪk/ adj. 流行的；传染性的（post-epidemic 后疫情时期的）

industry/ˈɪndəstri/ n. 产业；工业；勤勉

professor/prəˈfesə(r)/ n. 教授

*catering/ˈkeɪtərɪŋ/ n. (会议或社交活动的）饮食服务；酒席承办

amount/əˈmaʊnt/ n. 数量，数额；总数

\*triple/ˈtrɪpl/　v. 增至三倍

increase/ɪnˈkriːs/　v. 增加，提高；增强

**Phrases and Expressions**

transaction volume　交易额

on a yearly basis　每年（同比）

public vacation　公共假期

fit with　符合

tourism industry　旅游业

admission ticket　入场券；售票

sightseeing spot　旅游景点；观光名胜

**Proper Names**

National Day　国庆节

UnionPay　银联（China UnionPay 中国银联）

the Mid-Autumn Festival　中秋节

Tibet autonomous region　西藏自治区

Xinjiang Uygur autonomous region　新疆维吾尔自治区

Ningxia Hui autonomous region　宁夏回族自治区

Beijing Union University　北京联合大学

**Notes**

1. UnionPay card 即银联卡。2002年3月，经国务院同意，中国人民银行批准，在合并18家银行卡信息交换中心的基础上，由中国印钞造币总公司、中国工商银行、中国农业银行、中国银行、中国建设银行和交通银行等85家机构共同出资成立中国银联股份有限公司，总部设在上海。其主要负责建设和运营全国统一的银行卡跨行信息交换网络、提供银行卡跨行信息交换相关的专业化服务、管理和经营"银联"品牌、制定银行卡跨行交易业务规范和技术标准。

2. "On National Day, Oct.1, 2020, which overlapped with the Mid-Autumn Festival this year..." 表示"2020年10月1日国庆中秋双节当天，……"。2020年10月1日，星期四，农历八月十五。天文专家表示，中秋逢国庆是正常历法现象。"双节重逢"主要是因为闰月（2020年闰六月）。其次，本身中秋和国庆离得比较近，而两个节日都是法定节假日，有相应的假期，因此会有假期重合的情况发生，但并不多见。上一次出现在2009年10月3日（闰五月）。

3. "since the outbreak of the virus earlier this year" 表示"自今年早些时候新冠疫情爆发以来"。发生在2019年岁末2020年年初的新冠肺炎疫情，以汹汹来袭之势，深刻改变了2020年的春天，而最早遭受这一重大危机冲击与考验的中国，以巨大的魄力、惊人的壮举、勇毅的付出，最早阻断了疫情的传播，让这片土地成为世界上最安全最温暖

的家园。

4. "the Tibet autonomous region, Xinjiang Uygur autonomous region and Ningxia Hui autonomous region"指"西藏自治区、新疆维吾尔自治区、宁夏回族自治区"。自治区是在中国少数民族聚居地设立的省级民族区域自治地方，和省、直辖市同一级别。民族自治区在内部事务方面比其他省级行政区域有更多的自主权。我国另外两个民族自治区分别是内蒙古自治区、广西壮族自治区。

5. "the psychology of tourists to avoid crowds in the post-epidemic period"意为"后疫情时期游客避开人群的心理"。虽然疫情已经逐渐好转，但是防控依旧不得懈怠！人们还是要注意谨慎出行，尽量避开热闹的人群。

## Task 1  Answer the following questions according to the text.

1. How much did Chinese consumers spend on the first two days of the National Holiday by UnionPay card?

2. How much did the transaction volume recorded by UnionPay reach on Oct.1, 2020?

3. What kind of trips and tours have become more popular in the year 2020?

4. What are the advantages of tourism in western parts of China?

5. What's the psychology of tourists like in the post-epidemic period?

## Task 2  Choose the best answer for each of the following questions or statements according to the text.

1. Chinese consumers appear to be spending _____ during the National Day holiday than last year.
    A. less money                B. more money
    C. less time                 D. more time

2. On National Day, Oct.1, which overlapped with the Mid-Autumn Festival this year, transaction volume recorded by UnionPay reached 330 billion yuan, up _____, it found.
    A. 11.8 percent year-on-year         B. 11.8 percent on a yearly basis
    C. 15.5 percent on a yearly basis    D. 15.5 percent on a two-year basis

3. The rare extended National Day holiday has been _____ public vacation since the outbreak of the virus earlier this year.

A. the second shortest B. the shortest
C. the second longest D. the longest

4. The _____ were the areas that saw the fastest growth of spending on a yearly basis in the first two days, the UnionPay data found.

A. Tibet autonomous region B. Xinjiang Uygur autonomous region
C. Ningxia Hui autonomous region D. All above

5. What is this text mainly about?

A. Consumers spending up during the eight-day holiday.

B. Consumers liking trips and tours on National Day.

C. How to spend National Holiday every year.

D. Tourism in western parts of China this year.

## Task 3  动词化常用词缀（Common Affixes of Verbs）：

| | 词缀 | 位置 | 意义 | 例词 |
| --- | --- | --- | --- | --- |
| 动词化 | 前缀 be- | 加在名词、形容词前 | make intensive, make or become 使……加强，使……成为 | befriend, belittle, beware, besiege, beguile, belie, bequeath |
| | en-/em- | 加在名词、形容词前 | put into, make into 进入……之中，包围，使进入……状态 | embed, enlarge, enrich, enable, enlarge, endear, embrace, embed, embarrass, empower, embody |
| | -en | 加在名词、形容词后 | make or become, make into 使，变得 | strengthen, lengthen, harden, blacken, deepen, fasten, harden, thicken, weaken, broaden |
| | -ify | 加在名词、形容词、动词词根后 | turn into, make or become 转为，变为 | beautify, identify, magnify, clarify, modify, electrify, purify, simplify, certify |
| | 后缀 -ish | 加在动词词根后 | make or become 使，使成为，造成 | abolish, cherish, perish, flourish, finish |
| | -ize/-ise -yze/-yse | 加在形容词、动词词根后 | cause to be, make or become, treat in the way of 使，以……方式对待，……化 | realize, Americanize, democratize, popularize, analyze |
| | -ate | 加在动词词根后 | give or add, make or become 使起……作用，增加，做，造成 | activate, separate, operate, indicate, liberate |

# Unit 8　Consuming Habits

According to the word formation above, please match the prefixes or suffixes in column A with the words or roots in Column B to form correct verbs and write them down in Column C.

| Column A | Column B | Column C |
| --- | --- | --- |
| 1. be– | A. popular | |
| 2. en– | B. black | |
| 3. em– | C. beauti– | |
| 4. –en | D. ware | |
| 5. –ify | E. anal– | |
| 6. –ish | F. power | |
| 7. –ize/–ise | G. separ– | |
| 8. –yze/–yse | H. rich | |
| 9. –ate | I. cher– | |

# Part Ⅲ　Grammar Focus

## 定语从句（Attributive Clause）

修饰某一名词或者代词的从句叫定语从句。例如：
She is the woman whom/that I saw yesterday. 她就是我昨天见的那个女人。
They rushed over to help the man whose car had broken down. 那人车坏了，大家都跑过去帮忙。

### 一、定语从句也叫关系从句

跟定语从句相关的有两个最关键的词：先行词和关系词。被定语从句修饰的词叫先行词。引导定语从句的词叫关系词。

1. 关系词的分类。
（1）关系代词：　who（指代人，作主语或宾语）
　　　　　　　　whom（指代人，作宾语）
　　　　　　　　which（指代物，作主语或宾语）
　　　　　　　　that（指代人或物，作主语或宾语）
　　　　　　　　whose（=of whom/which 指代人或物，作定语）
（2）关系副词（作状语）：when（=in/at/on which 指代时间）
　　　　　　　　　　　　where（=in/at which 指代地点）
　　　　　　　　　　　　why（=for which 指代原因）

2. 关系词的功能。

$$\begin{cases} ①引导定语从句。\\ ②代替先行词。\\ ③在定语从句中担当一个句法成分。 \end{cases}$$

## 二、定语从句的分类

1. 限制性定语从句。

与先行词关系密切，如果没有定语从句，主句不完整，且与先行词之间无逗号。

e.g. I like the flowers (which/that) she grows. 我喜欢她种的花。

\* 注意：如果把后面的画线部分的限制性定语从句去掉，句子意思不完整。

2. 非限制性定语从句。

对先行词起补充说明作用，如果删除，主句意义仍然完整，与先行词之间有逗号。

\* 注意：that 不能用于非限制性定语从句。

e.g. On the desk there are some books, three of which are mine.

在书桌上有一些书，其中三本是我的。

My aunt Alice, whom I haven't seen for years, is coming next week.

我多年没见我的阿姨爱丽丝了，她下个星期要来。

\* 注意：去掉画线部分的非限制性定语从句，句子意思没有多大的影响。

## Task 1  Find out the following sentences in the text and underline the attributive clauses.

On National Day, Oct.1, 2020, which overlapped with the Mid-Autumn Festival this year, transaction volume recorded by UnionPay reached 330 billion yuan, up 15.5 percent on a yearly basis, it found.

The Tibet autonomous region, Xinjiang Uygur autonomous region and Ningxia Hui autonomous region were the areas that saw the fastest growth of spending on a yearly basis in the first two days, the UnionPay data found.

## Task 2  Choose the correct answer and underline the attributive clauses.

1. Is this the book _____ you borrowed from the library?
   A. what          B. that          C. who          D. whose
2. Do you know the man who _____ to Jack at the moment?
   A. has spoken    B. have spoken   C. is speaking  D. are speaking
3. This is the teacher from _____ we have learned a lot.
   A. whom          B. what          C. which        D. that
4. The factory _____ we are going to visit next week is not far from here.

| A. what | B. / | C. who | D. whose |

5. Have you brought the book _____ will be needed tomorrow?

| A. whom | B. what | C. that | D. who |

6. I like all music _____ I can dance to.

| A. that | B. what | C. whom | D. where |

7. The mobile phone, _____ he bought last year, is very useful.

| A. who | B. whom | C. which | D. that |

8. She likes musicians _____ write their own lyrics.

| A. who | B. which | C. what | D. whose |

9. She says that she'll never forget the time _____ she's spent working as a secretary in our company.

| A. which | B. when | C. why | D. where |

10. She says that she'll never forget the time _____ she works as a secretary in our company.

| A. which | B. when | C. why | D. where |

## Task 3  Make words together into a sentence and underline the attributive clauses.

1. may explain/asked her/have/the reason/for/that/her absence/you/?

_____

2. we/that/don't believe/has given/for/his being late/the reason/he/.

_____

3. why/tell me/the reason/yesterday/from the meeting/you/were absent/.

_____

4. they/and creative/the teacher/whose classes/are/very interesting/like/.

_____

5. works/the/tall and modern/building/I/where/my father/have been to/.

_____

## Part IV  Text 2

### Preview Questions

**Work in pairs and discuss the following questions.**

1. Do you know some authorities on consumer behavior? What are they about?
2. Talk about different market research surveys you've ever designed or read.

3. How do you see consumer preferences?

**Background Information**

1. About Simmons Market Research: Every year, tens of thousands of households participate in the National Consumer Survey, which gathers information on the lifestyles, media habits, and product/brand preferences of American families.

2. Privacy Pledge-Our Pledge to You: Simmons Market Research is committed to your privacy. We will NOT use your personal identifying information to advertise, promote, or market goods or services directly to you.

3. We are committed to representing the voice of all consumers. Our research helps American businesses keep their fingers on the pulse of the American consumer. Simmons considers the bond of privacy with our survey participants as our most important asset.

## WELCOME[①]

## Simmons Market Research

Since 1952, Simmons Market Research has been conducting high-quality research studies to find out how consumers in America spend their time.

We are nationally recognized as one of the leading authorities on the American consumer.

We invite you to learn more about our Simmons surveys, our commitment to our survey participants, and our mission to provide quality consumer behavior information while maintaining a strict privacy policy.

## YOUR VOICE COUNTS

## National Consumer Survey

This is an exciting opportunity for you to make your consumer preferences known.

It's your turn to make your voice heard by the companies who provide the products and services you use.

Whether it's where you shop, what you buy or what you're watching, reading or listening to-we want to hear from you!

## WHO WE ARE

## The Voice of the American Consumer ™

As one of the oldest and most respected authorities on consumer behavior, Simmons has been the Voice of The American Consumer ™ for more than 60 years.

Every year, more than 25,000 consumers participate in the National Consumer Survey,

---

① 本文摘自 Simmons Market Research 公司网站；原文网址 http://www.simmonssurvey.com/about-us.html

which gathers information on the lifestyles, media habits, and product/brand preferences of American families.

## WHAT WE DO

### National Consumer Survey

Simmons randomly selects households via a scientific process to represent communities across the country in our national research studies.

We ask households like yours to tell us about what they eat, what they read, watch and listen to, which activities they participate in, which products they buy, and how they feel about the consumer decisions they make every day.

## CONTACT US

### We would like to hear from you!

If you have any comments, suggestions or questions, call us toll-free, send us an E-mail or write to us. To help us answer your questions as quickly and accurately as possible, please provide a detailed description of your issue along with the address where we mailed your invitation/survey, or the phone number where we conducted the survey with you. This will help us get back to you faster.

**New Words**

conduct/kənˈdʌkt/  v. 组织；实施；进行
research/rɪˈsɜː(r)tʃ/  n. 研究；调查
*nationally/ˈnæʃnəlɪ/  adv. 全国性地；举国一致地
*recognized/ˈrekəɡnaɪzd/  adj. 公认的；经过验证的
authority/əˈθɔːrəti/  n. 权威；权力；当局（pl. authorities）
survey/ˈsɜː(r)veɪ/  n. 调查；测量；审视（pl. surveys）
commitment/kəˈmɪtmənt/  n. 承诺，保证；委托
mission/ˈmɪʃn/  n. 使命，任务；代表团
maintain/meɪnˈteɪn/  v. 维持；继续；维修
*preference/ˈprefrəns/  n. 偏爱，倾向；优先权
behavior/bɪˈheɪvjə(r)/  n. 行为，举止；态度
participate/pɑː(r)ˈtɪsɪpeɪt/  v. 参与，参加；分享
gather/ˈɡæðə(r)/  v. 收集；收割；使……聚集
brand/brænd/  n. 品牌，商标；类型
*randomly/ˈrændəmli/  adv. 随便地，任意地；无目的地
household/ˈhaʊshəʊld/  n. 一家人；一户

via /ˈvaɪə/   prep. 经由，通过；凭借
scientific /ˌsaɪənˈtɪfɪk/   adj. 科学的；系统的
represent /ˌreprɪˈzent/   v. 代表；表现；描绘
community /kəˈmjuːnəti/   n. 社区；共同体；团体（pl.communities）

## Phrases and Expressions

find out   找出，查明；发现
consumer behavior   消费者的行为
consumer preference   消费者偏好；消费偏爱
make...heard   使……被听到
hear from sb.   收到某人的来信
participate in   参加（活动）
across the country   遍布全国；祖国各地
consumer decision   消费决策

## Proper Names

Simmons Market Research   西蒙斯市场调查公司
National Consumer Survey   全国消费者调查

## Notes

1. call us toll-free：1-800-551-6425/1-800-822-4921（Hablamos espanol）

2. send us an E-mail：webcommentsms@mrisimmons.com

3. write to us：
Simmons Market Research（西蒙斯市场研究）
Attn：Director of National Consumer Survey（收件人：全国消费者调查中心）
800 Fairway Drive 800（度假屋）
Suite 295（295 套房）
Deerfield Beach，FL 33441（迪尔菲尔德海滩，佛罗里达 33441）
NY|Chicago|Deerfield Beach（纽约|芝加哥|迪尔菲尔德海滩）

## Multiple-Choice Questions

**Choose the best answer for each of the following questions or statements according to the text.**

1. What's the purpose of the high-quality research studies done by Simmons Market Research since 1952?

    A. To find out how consumers in America spend their time

    B. To learn more about their Simmons surveys

    C. To learn more about their commitment to their survey participants and their mission

D. To provide quality consumer behavior information
2. What information do Simmons surveys want to hear from consumers about their preferences?
   A. Where they shop
   B. What they buy
   C. What they're watching, reading or listening to
   D. All above
3. Which of the following is NOT true according to the text?
   A. Simmons is one of the oldest and most respected authorities on consumer behavior
   B. Simmons has been the Voice of The American Consumer™ for more than 60 years
   C. Less than 25,000 consumers participate in the National Consumer Survey every year
   D. Simmons gathers information on the lifestyles, media habits, and product/brand preferences of American families
4. Which of the following is NOT included in what households tell Simmons for national research studies?
   A. What they eat, read, watch and listen to
   B. How much they spend on daily necessities
   C. Which activities they participate in and which products they buy
   D. How they feel about the consumer decisions they make every day
5. What will the consumers be asked to do if they have any comments, suggestions or questions?
   A. To keep a secret
   B. To call Simmons toll-free, send them an E-mail or write to them
   C. To answer some questions slowly but accurately
   D. To prevent Simmons to get back to them faster

# Part V  Exercises

## Task 1  Vocabulary & Structure.

### Section A  Multiple Choice.

**Directions: Complete each one by deciding on the most appropriate word or words from the four choices.**

1. _____ a scientific process, we randomly select families throughout the country to represent people in their communities.
   A. To            B. Through           C. On            D. With
2. Once completed surveys _____, Simmons creates data that helps companies make better

products and services.

  A. are received    B. is received    C. receive    D. receives

3. Our research helps American businesses _____ their fingers on the pulse of the American consumer.

  A. keeps    B. keeping    C. keep    D. kept

4. The information you provide is used to bring you the _____ that you prefer and the _____ that you use in your local area.

  A. product, service      B. products, service

  C. product, services      D. products, services

5. It is also used to know _____ you like to watch on television, hear on the radio, read in newspapers and magazines and visit on the Internet.

  A. what    B. which    C. that    D. as

6. Simmons _____ all answers from participants into reports that are used by major U.S. companies.

  A. collects    B. continues    C. connects    D. combines

7. Your answers are never reported _____.

  A. individual      B. individuals

  C. individually      D. to be individual

8. For example, a report may look at _____ sporting events are attended by males in different areas of the country, or the department stores shopped most often by women.

  A. which    B. that    C. how    D. where

9. _____ you happen to fit into one of these groups, then your answers will be combined with the answers from other people in your group.

  A. Whether    B. If    C. Although    D. Even if

10. Below is _____ example of _____ report from a recent study.

  A. a, a    B. a, an    C. an, a    D. an, an

**Section B Blank Filling.**

  **Directions: There are five incomplete statements here. You should fill in the blanks with the proper forms of the words given in the brackets.**

11. We take the subject of consumer and respondent privacy very _____ (serious).

12. Our ability _____ (collect) accurate information on consumer preferences and attitudes depends largely on earning the trust of our survey respondents.

13. We safeguard your identity and _____ (person) information.

14. Simmons Market Research is a market research company; we are not direct _____ (market).

15. The National Consumer Survey _____ (mail) to a scientific national sample of

potential survey respondents next week.

## Task 2  Translation-English into Chinese.

**Directions**: This part, numbered 1 through 5, is to test your ability to translate English into Chinese. Each of the four sentences (No. 1 to No. 4) is followed by four choices of suggested translation marked A, B, C and D. Mark the best choice and circle the corresponding letter. Write your translation of the paragraph (No. 5) in the corresponding space on the Sheet.

1. Chinese consumers appear to be spending more money during the National Day holiday than last year.
   A. 今年,中国消费者在国庆节的消费支出比去年要多。
   B. 今年,中国消费者在国庆假期的消费支出比去年要多。
   C. 中国顾客今年在国庆期间的消费似乎不如去年多。
   D. 中国顾客今年在国庆节的消费似乎比去年多。

2. The rare extended National Day holiday has been the longest public vacation since the outbreak of the virus earlier this year.
   A. 这次罕见的国庆中秋长假是自今年早些时候新冠疫情爆发以来最长的公共假期。
   B. 这次罕见的国庆长假是自今年早些时候新冠疫情爆发以来最长的公共假期。
   C. 这次寻常的国庆中秋长假是自今年早些时候病毒爆发以来最长的公共假期。
   D. 这次寻常的国庆中秋长假是新冠疫情爆发以来最长的假期。

3. Long-distance trips and tours of western parts of China have seen growing popularity.
   A. 中国西部地区的长、短途旅行越来越受欢迎。
   B. 中国西部地区的长途旅行和旅游都在成长。
   C. 中国西部的长途旅行和旅游日益受到欢迎。
   D. 中国西部的长途旅游越来越受欢迎。

4. With vast land and lower population density, western China fits with the psychology of tourists to avoid crowds in the post-epidemic period.
   A. 中国西部地域辽阔,人口密度低,比较符合疫后游客的心理。
   B. 中国西部地域辽阔,人口密度低,比较符合疫后游客避开人群的心理。
   C. 中国西部地区土地辽阔,人口密度较低,符合后疫情时期游客避开人群的心理。
   D. 中国西部地区土地辽阔,人口密度不高,符合后疫情时期游客的心理。

5. On the first two days of the eight-day holiday, tourists' spending volume on hotels in Tibet more than doubled year-on-year, while spending on catering grew 49 percent. In Xinjiang, the amount spent on flight tickets tripled, and spending on admission tickets for sightseeing spots in Ningxia increased by 20 percent, according to UnionPay.

## Part Ⅵ　Writing: Complaint Letter（投诉信）

投诉信是客户对所提供的服务或购买的商品不满意时，向商家、机构提出相关的问题，并希望问题得到解决和处理所写的信件。这类信件的写作要点通常包括以下几个方面：

- 1. 对方的正式称谓，如某机构、某先生。
- 2. 提出写信的目的是抱怨或投诉。
- 3. 表明投诉的原因。
- 4. 向对方表示希望问题能够得到解决的意愿。
- 5. 留下自己的联系方式，以便能够得到回复。

### What is a Complaint Letter? [①]

You feel like complaining when you do not receive the things as per your desire. In businesses, people prefer to write a complaint letter when they feel disconnected towards a particular product or a company. Some of the people are afraid to write a complaint letter because they don't feel good to be argumentative. Understand that in such a letter you don't have to express your anger or show any kind of negativity. The complaint letter is a request for an adjustment and so you should write it accordingly. In this letter, you can describe mistakes, errors or any kind of damage that you have faced in the past.

Today, businesses are expanding overseas to a greater extent. Hence, unintentional mistakes are bound to happen and so you must know the right way to deal with it. As a buyer, if you are suffering from the bad quality of services or any kind of financial loss, then you have the right to complaint. The complaint letter is written in such a scenario to serve the purpose of complaint. It is important for you to make use of the polite tone while writing a complaint letter.

Things to Include in Your Complaint Letter!

When it comes to the complaint letter, here are the few things that you need to include:

---

① 本文摘自 Complaint Letter, Sample Complaint Letter Format；原文网址 https://www.letters.org/category/complaint-letter

- First, it is important for you to describe your problem appropriately.
- Once you are done with describing your problem, your next step will be to state the outcome that you are expecting out of the complaint letter.
- It is important for you to include dates related to purchases of goods or services.
- You should also include the date when the problem occurred.
- Describe, if any kind of action you have taken from your side to fix the problem.
- Describe the actions that you may take if the problem is not resolved.
- State the time by which you want the concerned authorities to revert back to you.
- If required, you can attach the supporting documents.

## New Words

*disconnected/ˌdɪskəˈnektɪd/　adj. 分离的；不连贯的；无系统的
particular/pərˈtɪkjələ(r)/　adj. 特别的；详细的；独有的
*argumentative/ˌɑːrɡjuˈmentətɪv/　adj. 好辩的；辩论的；争辩的
*negativity/ˌneɡəˈtɪvəti/　n. 否定性；消极性
adjustment/əˈdʒʌstmənt/　n. 调整，调节；调节器
*unintentional/ˌʌnɪnˈtenʃənl/　adj. 非故意的；无意识的
*scenario/səˈnɑːriəʊ, səˈnærioʊ/　n. 方案；情节；剧本；设想
tone/təʊn/　n. 语气；色调；音调；音色

## Phrases and Expressions

feel like (doing sth.)　想要做某事；喜欢做某事
as per　按照，依据；如同
to a greater extent　在较大程度上
deal with　处理；涉及；做生意
suffer from　忍受，遭受；患……病
financial loss　经济损失

## Task 1　Read the following complaint letter and two different replies to it. Discuss with your partner about the differences among them.①

Dear Sir or Madam,

　　I am sorry I have to say I was greatly disappointed with the inconvenient service you provided. You have sent the wrong goods, but the customer service paid no attention to my complaint. I'm very angry with your attitude for this irresponsible behavior. Now please reply to me soon to solve this problem.

---

① 本文摘自《连老外都在用的英语书信大全集》，朱子熹编著，中国纺织出版社2012年出版。

Best wishes,

Yours truly,<br>Lucy

**Reply 1:**

Dear Ms. Lucy,

  I am sorry to hear that. At the same time, thank you for bringing this matter to my attention. It is our oversight. We will exchange your goods immediately. Meanwhile, I won't hesitate to improve the service. I do hope that we can meet your full satisfaction next time.

Yours sincerely,<br>Mary

**Reply 2:**

Dear Ms. Lucy,

  We are sorry to learn from your letter and apologize for this matter. We must do our best to improve our service quality. But we can't meet your requirement while the time you raise the question has been out of limit. Please accept our sincere apologies for this mistake.

Sincerely yours,<br>Mary

## Task 2 Read the following complaint letter carefully and write two different replies to it. [①]

Dear Sir or Madam,

  The 10 sets of lamps we ordered were delivered yesterday, but we regretted that 3 sets were badly damaged.

  The packages containing the lamps appeared to be in good condition, so we accepted and signed for them without question. We unpacked the lamps with great care. So it can only assume that the damage must be due to careless handling at some stage prior to packing.

  We shall be glad if you will replace all 3 sets as soon as possible. Meanwhile, we have put the damaged sets aside in case you need to check them.

Best regards,

David

**Reply 1:**

---

[①] 本文摘自《连老外都在用的英语书信大全集》，朱子熹编著，中国纺织出版社 2012 年出版。

**Reply 2:**

### Task 3  Write a letter of complaint according to the given situation and prompts.

Write a letter of complaint to the manager of an online shopping website about the product(s) that you bought and aren't happy with. In your letter, you should do at least:

1. explain why you're writing the letter;
2. give details of your order;
3. describe the problem with the product(s);
4. say what you want the manager to do.

# 附 录

## Irregular Verbs of PRTCO B

### 英语 B 级考试不规则动词表

| Verb（动词原形） | Past tense（过去式） | Past participle（过去分词） |
|---|---|---|
| **A** | | |
| am/is 是 | was | been |
| are 是 | were | been |
| arise 出现；发生 | arose | arisen |
| awake 唤醒；醒来 | awoke/awakened | awoken |
| **B** | | |
| be 是 | was/were | been |
| bear 忍受 | bore | born/borne |
| beat 打；打败 | beat | beaten/beat |
| become 变得；变成 | became | become |
| begin 开始 | began | begun |
| bend 弯曲 | bent | bent |
| bet 赌；打赌 | bet/betted | bet/betted |
| bid 出价；投标 | bid | bid |
| bite 咬；咬伤 | bit | bitten |
| blow（风）吹 | blew | blown |
| break 打破；中断 | broke | broken |
| bring 带来 | brought | brought |
| broadcast 广播；播放 | broadcast | broadcast |
| build 建立 | built | built |
| burn 燃烧 | burnt/burned | burnt/burned |
| burst 爆发；爆炸 | burst | burst |
| buy 买；购买 | bought | bought |

| Verb（动词原形） | Past tense（过去式） | Past participle（过去分词） |
|---|---|---|
| **C** | | |
| catch 抓住；赶上 | caught | caught |
| choose 选择 | chose | chosen |
| come 来 | came | come |
| cost 花费 | cost | cost |
| cut 砍；割；切；剪 | cut | cut |
| **D** | | |
| deal 处理；交易 | dealt | dealt |
| dig 挖掘 | dug | dug |
| do | did | done |
| draw 画；拉；吸引 | drew | drawn |
| dream 做梦；梦想 | dreamt/dreamed | dreamt/dreamed |
| drink 喝；饮 | drank | drunk |
| drive 开车；驾驶 | drove | driven |
| **E** | | |
| eat 吃 | ate | eaten |
| **F** | | |
| fall 落下；跌倒 | fell | fallen |
| feed 喂养 | fed | fed |
| feel 感觉 | felt | felt |
| fight 打架；斗争 | fought | fought |
| find 找到；发现 | found | found |
| fit 合适；安装 | fit | fit |
| fly 飞；放飞 | flew | flown |
| forbid 禁止 | forbade | forbidden |
| forecast 预测；预报 | forecast | forecast |
| forget 忘记 | forgot | forgotten |
| forgive 原谅；饶恕 | forgave | forgiven |
| freeze 冷冻；冻结 | froze | frozen |
| **G** | | |
| get 得到 | got | got |
| give 给 | gave | given |

| Verb（动词原形） | Past tense（过去式） | Past participle（过去分词） |
| --- | --- | --- |
| go 去；走 | went | gone |
| grow 生长，成长；种植 | grew | grown |

## H

| Verb（动词原形） | Past tense（过去式） | Past participle（过去分词） |
| --- | --- | --- |
| hang 悬挂 | hung | hung |
| 绞死 | hanged | hanged |
| have/has 有；吃；喝；上课 | had | had |
| hear 听到；听见 | heard | heard |
| hide 隐藏；躲藏 | hid | hidden |
| hit 打；打击 | hit | hit |
| hold 持有；支持 | held | held |
| hurt 使受伤；伤害 | hurt | hurt |

## K

| Verb（动词原形） | Past tense（过去式） | Past participle（过去分词） |
| --- | --- | --- |
| keep 保持 | kept | kept |
| know 知道；认识；了解 | knew | known |

## L

| Verb（动词原形） | Past tense（过去式） | Past participle（过去分词） |
| --- | --- | --- |
| lay 放置；产卵 | laid | laid |
| lead 领导；引导 | led | led |
| lean 倾斜；倚靠 | leaned/leant | leaned/leant leap |
| learn 学习；得知 | learned/learnt | learned/learnt |
| leave 离开；留下 | left | left |
| lend 借给 | lent | lent |
| let 让 | let | let |
| lie 躺；位于 | lay | lain |
| 说谎；撒谎 | lied | lied |
| light 照亮；点燃 | lit/lighted | lit/lighted |
| lose 丢失；失去 | lost | lost |

## M

| Verb（动词原形） | Past tense（过去式） | Past participle（过去分词） |
| --- | --- | --- |
| make 使；让 | made | made |
| mean 意思是；想要 | meant | meant |
| meet 遇见；遇到 | met | met |
| mistake 弄错；误解 | mistook | mistaken |

| Verb(动词原形) | Past tense(过去式) | Past participle(过去分词) |
| --- | --- | --- |
| **O** | | |
| overcome 克服 | overcame | overcome |
| **P** | | |
| pay 付款；支付 | paid | paid |
| prove 证明；证实 | proved | proven/proved |
| put 放 | put | put |
| **Q** | | |
| quit 离开；放弃 | quit/quitted | quit/quitted |
| **R** | | |
| read 读；看（书、报） | read/red/ | read/red/ |
| ride 骑（马、自行车） | rode | ridden |
| ring 按铃；打电话 | rang | rung |
| rise 上升；增强 | rose | risen |
| run 跑；运营 | ran | run |
| **S** | | |
| say 说；讲 | said | said |
| see 看见；看到 | saw | seen |
| seek 寻找；寻求 | sought | sought |
| sell 卖；销售 | sold | sold |
| send 寄；发送；派遣 | sent | sent |
| set 放，置；树立 | set | set |
| sew 缝纫；缝合 | sewed | sewn/sewed |
| shake 摇动；颤抖 | shook | shaken |
| shine 照耀；发光 | shined/shone | shined/shone |
| shoot 射击；发射 | shot | shot |
| show 显示；说明；展出 | showed | shown/showed |
| shut 关上；闭上 | shut | shut |
| sing 唱；唱歌 | sang | sung |
| sit 坐；就座 | sat | sat |
| sleep 睡觉 | slept | slept |
| slide （使）滑动 | slid | slid |

| Verb（动词原形） | Past tense（过去式） | Past participle（过去分词） |
| --- | --- | --- |
| smell 嗅；闻到；闻起来 | smelled/smelt | smelled/smelt |
| speak 说话；演讲 | spoke | spoken |
| speed 加速 | sped/speeded | sped/speeded |
| spell 拼；拼写 | spelled/spelt | spelled/spelt |
| spend 花费；度过 | spent | spent |
| split 劈开；裂开 | split | split |
| spread 传播；伸展 | spread | spread |
| stand 站立；忍受 | stood | stood |
| steal 偷；窃取 | stole | stolen |
| stick 粘住，粘贴；坚持 | stuck | stuck |
| strike 罢工 | struck | stricken |
| strike 打；击（=hit） | struck | struck/stricken |
| sweep 打扫；清扫 | swept | swept |
| swim 游泳 | swam | swum |

## T

| Verb（动词原形） | Past tense（过去式） | Past participle（过去分词） |
| --- | --- | --- |
| take 拿（走）；取；抓 | took | taken |
| teach 教；教授；讲授 | taught | taught |
| tear 流泪；撕破 | tore | torn |
| tell 告诉；说；讲述 | told | told |
| think 想；认为 | thought | thought |
| throw 扔；掷 | threw | thrown |

## U

| Verb（动词原形） | Past tense（过去式） | Past participle（过去分词） |
| --- | --- | --- |
| understand 懂得；了解 | understood | understood |
| upset 打翻；扰乱 | upset | upset |

## W

| Verb（动词原形） | Past tense（过去式） | Past participle（过去分词） |
| --- | --- | --- |
| wake 醒来；唤醒 | woke/waked | woken/waked |
| wear 穿，戴；用旧 | wore | worn |
| win 赢得；获胜 | won | won |
| withdraw 收回；撤销 | withdrew | withdrawn |
| write 写，写作；写信 | wrote | written |